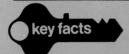

Key Facts Colour Guide

SAILING

Barry Pickthall

Cassell
London

ACKNOWLEDGEMENTS

All photographs are by Barry Pickthall, except those listed below:

Colour Library International, back cover; Picture-point, page 11.

Diagrams by P.A.G. Milne.

CASSELL LTD.
35 Red Lion Square, London WC1R 4SG
and at Sydney, Auckland, Toronto, Johannesburg,
an affiliate of
Macmillan Publishing Co., Ltd.,
New York.

Designed and produced for Cassell Ltd. by
Intercontinental Book Productions,
Berkshire House, Queen Street,
Maidenhead, Berkshire, SLF INF.

Copyright © 1980 Intercontinental Book Productions

First published 1980

ISBN 0 304 30684 3

Printed in Hong Kong

Contents

All about Dinghies and Cruisers

To the beginner it all looks such fun – those busy harbour scenes with yachts creaming along through the water, heeled hard over at an angle, and dinghies chasing each other round crowded marks. By contrast, you can visualize the peace of the solitary craft swinging at anchor in some quiet, secluded cove.

First thoughts about sailing will always conjure up brilliant sunshine, blue skies, and calm seas. Those gale force winds, lashing rain, and rough seas seem a million miles away. And yet the fact that they may not be so remote should not put you off. Sailing any size of craft can be relaxing in almost any weather. That old maxim, 'a change is as good as a rest', could not be more true than with this sport. Relaxation comes not from a lazy day at the helm but from the change of scenery as you sail along, and the sense of achievement: first learning to steer the boat, then taking her through the harbour entrance, and later heading out for anchorages new.

But the sea holds many perils for the unwary, and when buying a boat for the first time a vague interest in getting afloat is not enough. You have to be quite certain of what you want, and the only way to do this is to gain some experience first. If you have friends who sail, ask them to take you along. If not, enrol at a nearby sailing school and learn the basics there. No amount of reading will teach you the finer points, for, with sailing, experience is everything.

Which Boat to Buy

It can be unwise to ask your friends which boat to buy, for however knowledgeable they seem their words of advice may not be soundly based on experience. While you may hanker after a small craft to potter around in, you could finish up with a performance boat which would scare the living daylights out of both you and everyone else on the water!

If you are going sailing with friends get a full season under your belt first, so that you really know what you can handle and what is suitable to your needs. If you take lessons, the instructor will be the best person to advise you.

Sailing, a cynic once said, was 'more akin to tearing up £5 notes under a cold shower'. While he may have been right about the cold shower, the costs for sailing craft, at least, need not be exhorbitant. Indeed, once the capital outlay for the boat has been made, the sport need be no more expensive than golf. Well maintained boats, whatever their size, will rarely depreciate in value, and the more popular types may well appreciate to provide an excellent hedge against inflation.

Most sailing schools use dinghies for instruction afloat and there is a great deal of sense in this, for whatever the size of boat, the principles of sailing are the same. Even if what you are really looking for is a family cruiser to start with, it will make no difference if you learn to sail in a dinghy. Once you can handle one of these confidently the move up will be easy to make.

Cruisers come in all shapes and sizes and for a beginner the choice can be daunting. A fin keel boat could well give the best all round performance but the advantage of bilge keels – they allow the boat to sit upright when taking the ground – soon becomes apparent if you go exploring muddy creeks and distant beaches. Yachts with centreplates that can be hauled up and down may at first seem to offer the best of both worlds. But some designs are tender and likely to heel more readily than their heavier ballasted fixed-keel counterparts.

To maintain continuity we have chosen the 27 ft Salty Dog designed by Peter Milne to illustrate many of the points concerned

Sailing through the Solent. This X Boat is just one of many early One-design keel boat classes still popular today.

4

with sailing cruisers. Moulded in glass fibre, this design is typical of modern cruisers to be found the world over. She has a simple sloop rig set on alloy spars and is available with either fin or bilge keel configurations. The dinghy illustrations show the ubiquitous 10 ft Mirror, one of the fastest growing classes, with examples to be found in most sailing countries of the world. Designed by Barry Bucknell and Jack Holt for amateur construction in plywood, this snub-nosed dinghy which has provided a start into sailing for thousands of families and children, is an ideal trainer. It is also an excellent boat to illustrate here for the design embodies the many facets of almost all other small dinghies. The simple gunter rig with its gaff hoist is set up in a similar way to most other fractional dinghy plans and the progression from here to setting up a basic bermudian rig is simple enough. The Mirror's basic daggerboard arrangement which resists sideways drift is another idea found in many other designs and though other more sophisticated boats may have boards that pivot, the principle remains the same.

The Scamp pram dinghy, designed by Peter Milne, is an ideal junior trainer.

Joining a Club

If a dinghy is more in your line than a cruiser, it is a good idea to join a yacht club before going on to buy a boat of your own. These clubs usually support specific dinghy classes, ones that are best suited to the sailing conditions in their locality; and should you think of buying one of these dinghies, it could well prove a passport to membership. Whatever the case, go and have a chat over the bar – these clubs are friendly places and the members will naturally know all about sailing in the area. Some may even be able to help you to find a second-hand craft.

Wood or Glass Fibre Hulls

But what type of construction is best – wood or glass fibre?

The dinghy purists amongst us will say that there is nothing better than wood: 'It's a much stiffer material and makes a more competitive boat.' But then the purists also relish the rubbing down and repainting each year! However, you shouldn't imagine that glass fibre is totally maintenance free either. After a few seasons' use, some of these boats need painting, too.

In the case of dinghies, glass fibre boats are often a little cheaper than their wooden counterparts, and, with modern technology they can be built as strong as wooden craft. It's really a question of personal choice.

However, when we move up to larger craft new wooden cruisers are few and far between, glass fibre being a much more economical material to build with. If you are looking at second-hand boats for the first time, it is often best to work through reputable brokers but if nothing else, take a knowledgeable friend along with you to poke around and find any faults. You would never buy a house without first reading a surveyor's report and it should be the same with a boat, especially one that is a few years old. The surveyor's fees may seem expensive, but his report could save you a lot of trouble and money in the long run. Buying a boat should never be rushed. The answer is always to get some sailing experience first so

The Southerly 28 is a typical family cruiser suitable for first time buyers.

that you know what you are looking for, and then to take all the time and trouble you need to find exactly that.

Secure a berth

A vacant mooring, especially in one of the more popular harbours, can be difficult to acquire – some marinas now have extensive waiting lists. It might therefore be prudent to find a berth first, then choose a suitable cruiser to fit it. The best place to make enquiries about the availability of berths is at the Harbour Master's office. This office will usually be the first to hear of any vacancies. If all that is available is a mooring that dries out at low water, it will be no good buying a fin keeled craft because it will fall on its side at every tide. However, many boat builders produce two or more versions of their craft, with bilge keels designed to allow the boat to sit upright on the ground as an option. Before buying, though, it is always wise to check that the boat really will stand up on its own feet.

Sailing Around the World

While ideas on sailing vary little around the world, conditions can provide a considerable contrast. There is little to match the strong currents and high rise and fall of tides in Britain, while the Great Lakes of North America are, in English eyes, seas in their own right. But one common factor, the bond of friendship which sailing engenders, leaves no yachtsman without a port of refuge anywhere in the world.

Rigs and Parts of the Boat

At first sight, the many rigs may seem confusing, but today most designers have standardized their thoughts on three or four types of rig.

Which Rig is Best?

Most dinghies are either gunter rigged, like the popular Mirror, or drawn with a Bermudian sail plan. The advantage of the gunter rig, especially with small boats, is that when packed down for trailing or car-topping the spars are short enough to fit inside the boat. The disadvantage is that it takes longer to set up and is less efficient than the Bermudian sail plan, which is now by far the most popular rig on dinghies.

Sloop rig

With cruisers and large sailing yachts there is more choice of rig than with dinghies, but the Bermudian sloop is the most popular. This is because it is one of the simplest, having only a mainsail and foresail set on one mast, which requires the minimum of rigging.

It is also an easy sail plan for crews to handle.

Cutter rig

Another single-masted rig, this was popular at the beginning of the century, and many of these yachts were fitted with a bow sprit. Compared with a sloop, a cutter has two headsails (forestay sail and jib) which individually are smaller and therefore more manageable. However, the cutter is a more complex and expensive rig than a sloop.

Ketch rig

The most popular of the two masted rigs, this is often seen on large cruisers that boast a centre cockpit and aft cabin. The aftermost mast is always stepped forward of the rudder post and the sail that is set from it is known as the mizzen. It is an easy sail plan to handle, especially on large yachts, since the sail area is divided into three which makes it easier to reef down in heavy weather.

Yawl rig

The main difference between a ketch and a yawl is the position of the mizzen mast. The

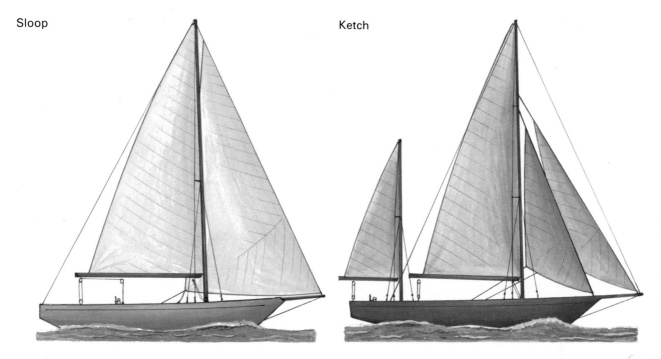

Sloop

Ketch

mizzen of a yawl is set abaft the rudder post and is often smaller in area than that of a ketch of equivalent size.

Schooner rig

Schooners are a rare sight today. This rig has two masts with the foremast normally shorter than the main mast, though they are sometimes of the same height. Two sails are usually carried between the masts. The lower is known as a staysail, the upper, a fisherman's staysail.

Gaff rig

The gaff rig was popular amongst working sailboats at the turn of the century and many examples are still afloat today. The rig is so called because of the heavy gaff boom which supports the head of the sail and goes to and pivots on the mast. Because of their bulk, these boats rarely sailed well to windward, and skippers would often wait for a beam or following wind before starting a voyage. It is on these points of sail that the low aspect gaff rig is most powerful because it has a much lower heeling moment than its taller Bermudian counterpart.

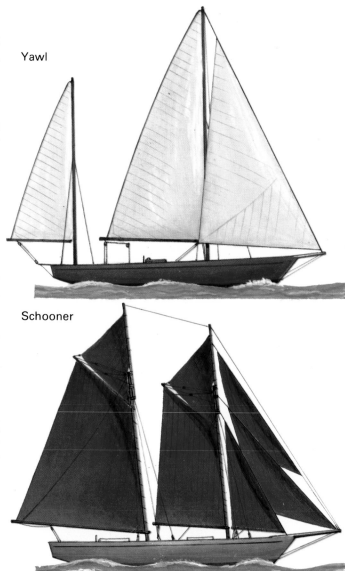

Yawl

Schooner

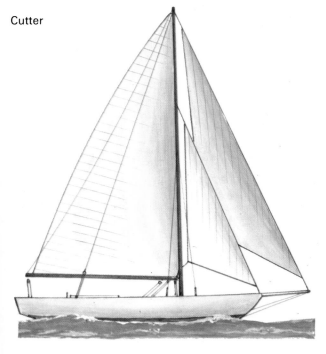

Cutter

Gaff-rigged Cutter

The illustrations show a Mirror dinghy and a Salty Dog cruiser, listing all the rigging, warps and parts of the boat. The best way to memorize it all is to test yourself and the crew during quiet moments at home.

1 Rudder
2 Mooring cleats
3 Tiller
4 Pushpit
5 Cockpit
6 Safety lines
7 Foresail winches and cleats
8 Backstay
9 Steering compass
10 Navigation instruments
11 Halyard winch and cleats
12 Tack downhaul
13 Kicking strap
14 Main sheet
15 Foresail sheets
16 Clew outhaul
17 Clew
18 Topping lift
19 Boom
20 Tack
21 Reefing points
22 Mast
23 Luff
24 Leech
25 Spreader
26 Foresail hanks
27 Forestay
28 Shrouds
29 Inner forestay
30 Foresail
31 Pulpit
32 Foresheet block
    and track
33 Stanchion
34 Toerail
35 Fin keel
36 Outboard
    motor bracket

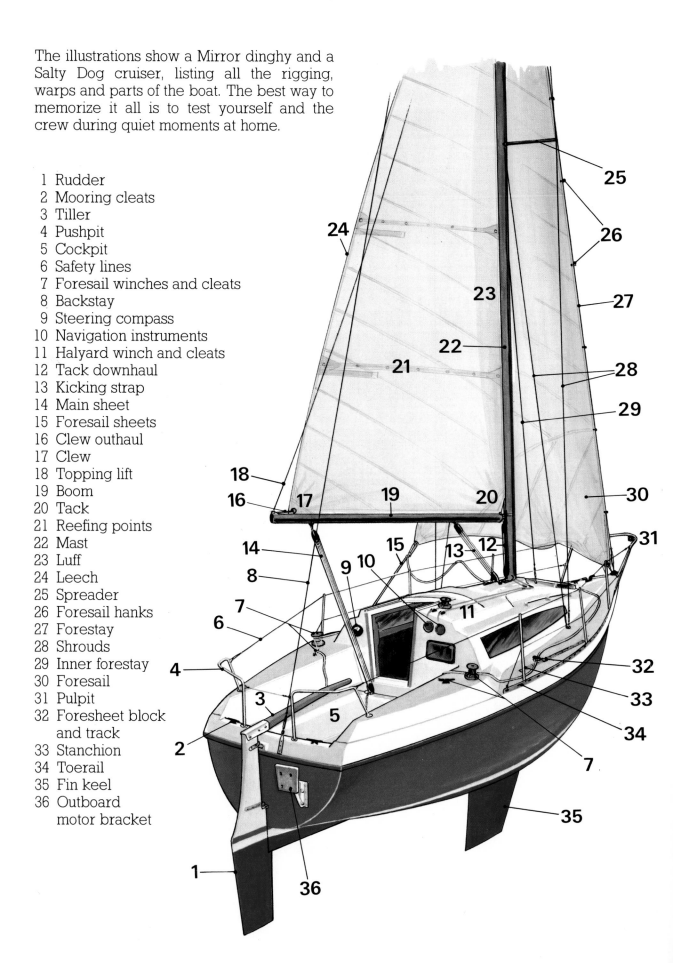

1 Buoyancy tanks
2 Forward mast step (for sailing single-handed with mainsail only)
3 Jib tack
4 Jib
5 Mainsail lashing
6 Shrouds
7 Gaff jaws
8 Jib hanks
9 Jib halyard
10 Mast
11 Mainsail halyard
12 Gaff
13 Burgee
14 Peak
15 Sail battens and pockets
16 Leech
17 Boom
18 Mainsheet
19 Lifting rudder
20 Tiller
21 Tiller extension
22 Fairlead
23 Jib sheets
24 Daggerboard
25 Elastic friction cord
26 Thwart
27 Daggerboard case
28 Gooseneck
29 Tack
30 Kicking strap
31 Luff

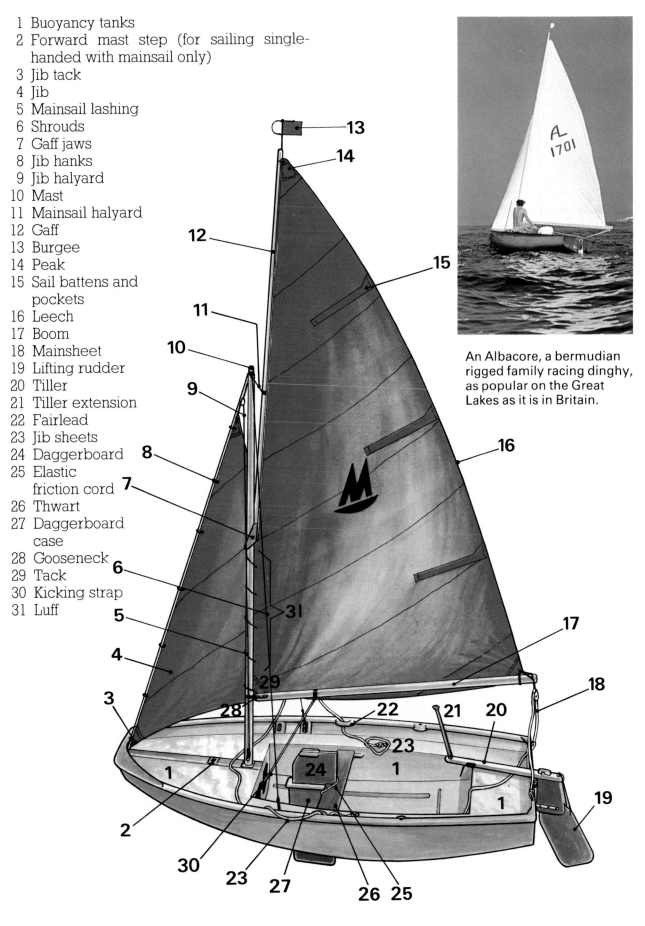

An Albacore, a bermudian rigged family racing dinghy, as popular on the Great Lakes as it is in Britain.

Harnessing the Wind

There is no need to get oneself totally bogged down with the theory of sailing at this early stage. All one does have to learn is the effect that the wind has on a boat when the set or position of the sails are altered.

Airflow across the Mainsail

Imagine for a moment that your boat is lying at 90 degrees to the wind with the boom free and sail flapping as in Fig 1.

If the sheet is pulled in slightly it can be seen from Fig 2 that the sail begins to fill, catching the wind along the leech or aft edge.

Pull the sheet in further and more of the sail takes up its designed aerofoil shape until finally the sail stops flapping altogether, as shown in Fig 3. This is when the sail is developing maximum forward thrust.

Pull the sheet in too much however, and the airflow starts to break down on the leeward side of the sail as shown in Fig 4. Here the sail is starting to stall, generating less power than in Fig 3 whilst presenting a greater area to the wind, thus making the boat want to heel more.

It is often best for beginners to start sailing using just the mainsail, for it takes time and experience before a sailor can read and understand that invisible flow of air across the sail.

First he or she must learn to judge the direction of the wind by watching the catspaws creating their own individual wavelets on the surface of the water; watching flags fluttering and the effect the wind is having on the course and set of other sailng craft close by; but most of all, by watching the burgee set at the masthead which shows the exact angle the apparent wind is blowing across the sail. Only when the beginner learns to gauge the wind direction from the tell-tale signs around and to sense when the sail is set correctly should he begin to worry about the jib. Sailing is like riding a bicycle. It takes

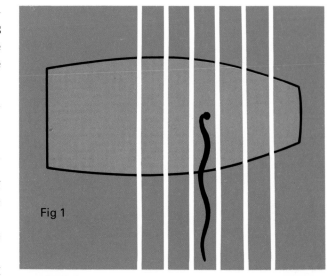

Fig 1

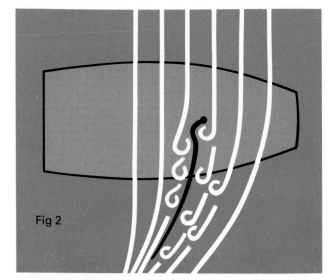

Fig 2

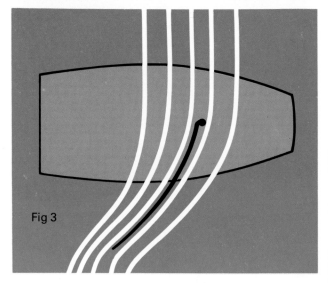

Fig 3

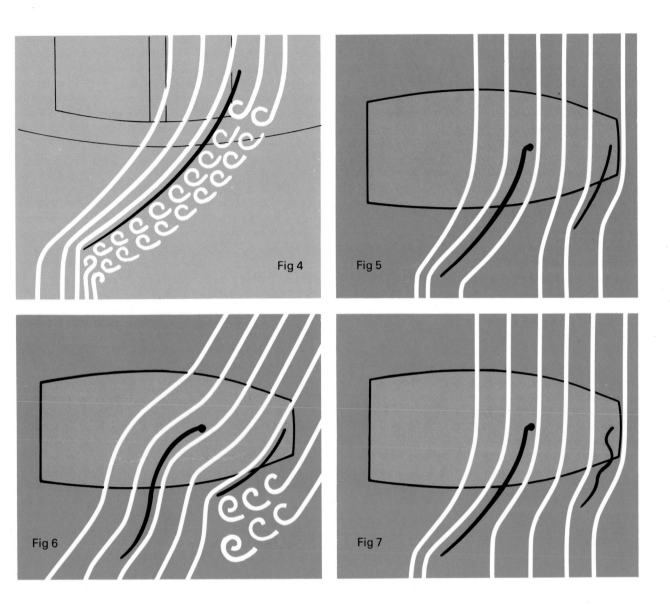

Fig 4

Fig 5

Fig 6

Fig 7

time to learn the basics, but once grasped, it is an instinct that is never lost.

Mainsail and Jib Set Together

The jib not only provides extra power to the rig but gives a better balance, making the boat easier to manoeuvre. However these benefits are only obtained when the two sails are adjusted in unison at the same angle to the wind so that the air flow remains smooth over both as is shown in Fig 5.

If the jib is sheeted in too tightly (as it is in Fig 6) not only does the airflow start to break down on the leeward side as it does with the sail in Fig 4, but it also destroys the airflow across the mainsail. Indeed, the effect

it has is to choke the slot between the two sails.

If however the jib is not sheeted in tight enough as in Fig 7, it will flap along the leading edge just as the mainsail does in Fig 2, adding little if any extra power to the rig.

Making a Course to Windward

A rig will not generate any forward power when set higher than 45 degrees to the wind depending on the design of boat.

When sailing to a point directly windward therefore, your boat has to make a zigzag course which is known as *beating to windward* (Fig 8). It is when sailing on this course that the sails have to be pulled in as tight as possible. Sailing in this state is known as *sailing close hauled*.

Should the boat be pointed too high into the wind then both the jib and mainsail will begin to flutter along their luffs as shown in Fig 9 and the rig will not generate so much forward power. Sailing a course too high into the wind is called *pinching to windward*.

If on the other hand the bow is turned away from the wind this is known as *bearing away* and if a lower course is held for any length of time, then obviously more zigzag changes of course will be needed to reach that goal to windward. These changes of course, when the bow passes through the eye of the wind are known as *tacks*.

There is a great deal of side force generated by the rig when sailing to windward. This can only be counteracted by the daggerboard or centreboard in a dinghy or the drop keel in a cruiser if it has one, which should always be in the fully down position – otherwise the boat will only slew sideways making no forward gains at all.

Sailing Across the Wind

Steering the boat at a slightly larger angle to the wind is called *sailing on a close reach* (Fig 10).

When the wind is at an angle of 90 degrees to the boat's course, the fastest point of sailing, it is *sailing on a beam reach* (Fig 11).

If the course set is at an even wider angle to the wind this is called *sailing on a broad reach* (Fig 12).

Airflow across the sails when the boat is beating to windward.

Sailing Downwind

When the boat is turned to a point where the wind is astern, this is known as *running before the wind* (Fig 13).

When sailing at this attitude to the wind little attention need be paid to the airflow across the sails for the wind merely pushes the boat along. It is best therefore to have the two sails set on opposite sides to each other to present the maximum area. This is *running before the wind goosewinged*.

Points to Remember

Remember that the sheets must be eased to match the sails to every change of course away from the wind otherwise they will stall.

If the boat is headed higher into the wind then the opposite is the case.

As the bows bear away from the wind to reduce drag, the daggerboard/centreplate can be raised a little at a time, to the point where it is almost fully housed when running before the wind.

Fig 8

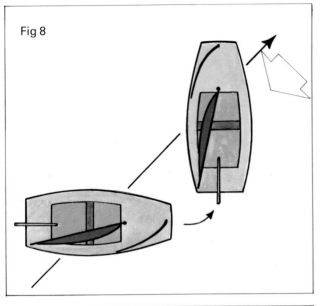

Fig 9

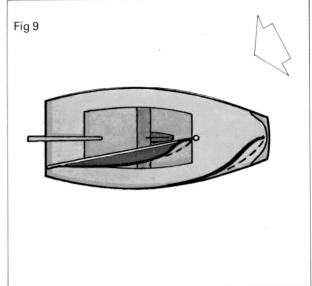

Fig 10

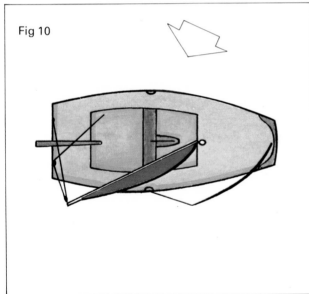

Fig 11

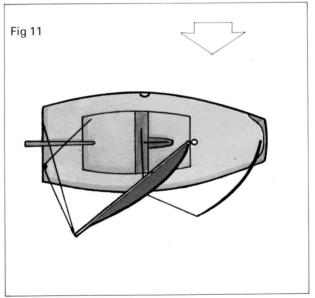

Fig 12

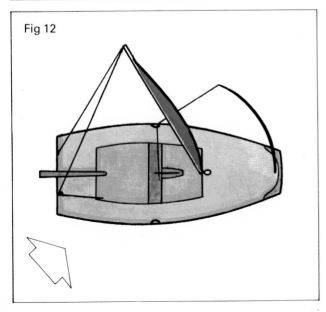

Fig 13

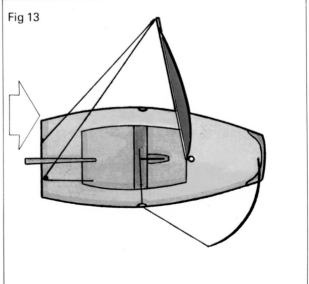

Making Ready

The first job is to rig the boat – this entails hoisting sails and generally getting ready to set off.

Most small dinghies will be rigged ashore and then pushed into the water on their launching trollies. Trailer cruisers have their masts stepped ashore but it is always best to launch the boat and move out to an empty patch of water to anchor, or pick up a spare mooring before hoisting sails.

The wheel bearings on most road trailers are not waterproof and you run the risk of them seizing up if they are ever immersed. It is wise to carry a spare set of bearings with you when trailing just in case, but most chandlers stock waterproofing kits which are cheap and will alleviate the problem altogether.

Bending On The Sails

Before the headsail is hoisted the jib tack must be attached to its tack fitting which is at the base of the forestay; the hanks fitted to the luff of the sail are clipped on to the stay, and the sheets are attached to the clew. The

Setting the jib:
Fig 1: The jib hanks attached to the luff of the sail are slotted on to the forestay and twisted to lock.
Fig 2: Once all the hanks are attached the jib halyard is shackled to the head of the sail.
Fig 3: The tack of the jib is shackled to a plate on the bow which is often also used for the forestay attachment.
Setting the mainsail:
Fig 4: Here the luff of the mainsail is being fed into the groove cut in the gaff.
Fig 5: Then the peak of the mainsail is tied off at the outer end.
Fig 6: The Mirror has a loose-footed mainsail, which is attached to the boom at the tack and clew outhaul (outer end of boom).
Fig 7: The gaff is now attached to the mast and locked in place with an elastic cord. Once hoisted, the loose luff is laced to the mast.
Fig 8: The final job before hoisting is to fit the battens in their pockets, making sure that the thin end is fitted first.

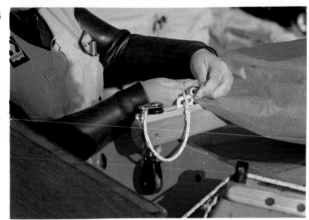

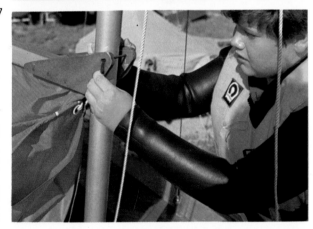

luff of the sail has to be pulled taut when hoisting again, either with a winch or by hand. If it is left slack, the sail will sag off and badly affect the boat's pointing ability to windward.

The next job is to attach the mainsail to the boom. With most metal spars, the foot of the sail has to be fed into a slot running along the top of the boom and then made fast at both clew and tack positions. The boom will normally have a black band painted around it at the outboard end, indicating the limit to which the sail may be stretched out. In light weather when there is little wind to fill it out, it may help the sail to set better if the clew is allowed to lie an inch or more inside the black band to reduce creases. With the Mirror dinghy, however, the sail is cut with a loose foot which is attached to the boom only at tack and clew.

Next, the main halyard is attached to the headboard of the sail and the bolt rope or slides sewn to the luff are fed into the track on the aft side of the mast as the sail is hoisted.

Some masts are fitted with a gooseneck (the swivel joint between boom and mast) which adjusts vertically. This should be released and, with the boom fitted, pushed to its upper limit so that the sail can be hoisted right to the top of the mast without stretching the luff. Most masts will have a painted band at the top, just like that painted on the boom, to show how far the sail may be pulled up.

Once the halyard has been made off on the cleat, the gooseneck can be pulled down to stretch the luff. Again, a black band is normally painted around the mast – this one level with the gooseneck position – to show the limit to which the luff may be stretched. The sail can be set an inch or so up from the band in light weather to take out any creases up the luff.

With masts that do not have an adjustable gooseneck, the halyard has to be tensioned, either with a winch or by hand.

On the gunter-rigged Mirror there is a bolt rope on the sail which slides along the gaff and the sail is hoisted with the halyard attached to this spar. However, the luff of the sail between boom and gaff has to be laced to the mast.

Hoisting Sails Afloat

The most important point is to ensure that the boat lies head to wind and sheets are left free, otherwise the sails will fill and the boat will be uncontrollable.

I find it best to work to a standard procedure – that way nothing is overlooked. My own mental check list runs like this:–

1. Check that the rudder blade is in the down position and that the tiller is free to move.

2. Hoist the burgee – triangular for cruising, square for racing.

3. Bend on the sails. This is a term which means getting the sails ready to hoist, with battens in their pockets (tapered end first), mainsail attached to the boom, jib hanks clipped on the forestay and halyards attached.

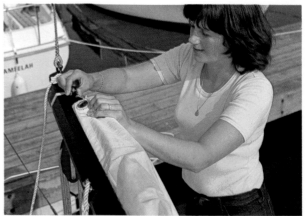

4. Hoist sails. It is normally best to hoist the smallest first; with a dinghy this will be the jib, but with a keel boat the mainsail is often the smaller.

5. Tighten the kicking strap.

Cruiser – Bending on mainsail:
Fig 9: The first job is to slide the foot of the mainsail into its groove on top of the boom, feeding the clew into the opening close to the gooseneck.
Fig 10: Now the clew is shackled to the outhaul at the opposite end of the boom, ensuring that it does not go beyond the marker band.
Fig 11: Battens are slotted into their pockets.
Fig 12: Some cruisers simply have a bolt-rope on the luff of the mainsail which is fed up a slot in the mast. On larger yachts slides are used to attach sail to mast and are fed individually into the luff groove.
Bending on headsail:
Fig 13: The tack is shackled either direct down onto the bow fitting or via a strop used to heighten the sail.
Fig 14: The luff is hanked to the forestay.
Fig 15: Headsail halyard is attached.
Fig 16: Sheets are tied to the clew using bowline knots . . . and the sails are then ready for hoisting.

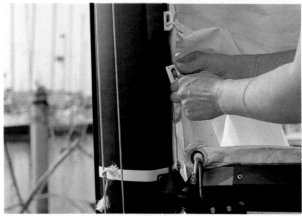

6. Stand by to cast off from the mooring.

7. Make sure that the sheets are free, letting the sails flap. Never try to hold the boom – just keep that head ducked!

Hoisting Sails Ashore

1. Point the boat head to wind and as close to the water's edge as possible. If the rudder blade is not a fixed type and can be hoisted, it can be fitted to the transom and the tiller fixed in the rudder head.

2. Hoist the burgee.

3. Bend on the sails.

4. Hoist the mainsail.

5. Hoist the jib tight. Remember that the narrowest corner of the sail is the head and it is easier if the sheets are attached to the clew before the sail is hoisted.

6. Check that the drain bungs are firmly in their sockets.

7. Push the boat into the water, making sure that it still heads into the wind.

8. Recover the launching trolley and remember to haul it above the high tide mark, otherwise it might float away before you return.

9. Let the crew aboard and make ready with the centreboard or daggerboard so that it can be pushed down as soon as there is sufficient water.

10. Release the uphaul rope on the rudder blade.

11. Push the boat out and climb aboard. The crew sheets in the jib and pushes down the centreboard (daggerboard) while the helmsman pulls the rudder blade right down and secures it. Don't pull in the mainsheet until these points have been completed.

Handling a Boat

Sailing is very much like riding a bicycle – it takes time to learn balance and control but, once mastered, it is a skill never forgotten. Both steering and crewing a sail boat is very much a question of balance and control. There is never any need for rushed or jerky movements and you rarely need to push the tiller across more than 30 degrees from centre, even for the tightest manoeuvre. Pushed over any further, the rudder blade may stall and be ineffective, especially if the boat is going astern.

Going About

The first manoeuvre you learn is tacking through the eye of the wind when sailing a zigzag course to windward. This is termed going about. The secret is not to rush things, especially when you are beginning. Within reason, the more time the boat takes to cross from one tack to another, the more chance you have of making a success of it.

The helmsman calls 'ready about' when

When going about, don't rush things. The helmsman must always call out 'ready about' to prepare his crew and 'lee-oh' signals the start of the manoeuvre.

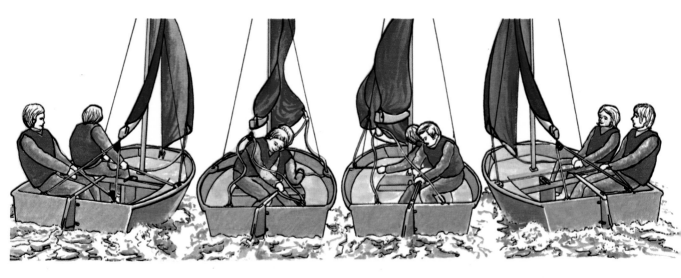

it is time to put in a tack, but this is merely a warning for the crew to be prepared. 'Lee-oh' is the call made at the start of the turn.

The helmsman, who normally sits on the windward side so that he can see ahead, pushes the tiller down and away from him to bring the bow through the eye of the wind, and the crew releases the jib sheets. Once the boom swings in towards the centreline of the boat, the helmsman moves across to the other side while the crew crouches inside to balance the boat. Once across, the helmsman has to change tiller and sheet over in his hands and the crew takes hold of the opposite jib sheet.

When the boat has turned through the wind the crew pulls the jib sheet across – but it should never be pulled in tight until the sail starts to fill, otherwise it will just backwind and push the bow round on to the old tack again. Wait for it to start filling, then climb across to the weather side, sheeting in as you go. It is the crew's job to balance the boat and in very light weather it may be necessary to stay on the opposite side from the helmsman to balance his weight.

Altering Course to a Run

You have now reached your windward goal, and want to return to the starting point by

When bearing away, the rig loses much of its heeling force; the crew must be ready to move inboard to balance the boat.

While the helmsman pushes the helm down and swops sides, the crew's job is to balance the boat and pull the jib sheets across as the boat passes through the eye of the wind.

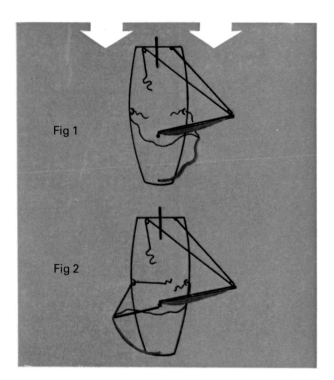

Running before the wind, goosewinged:
Fig 1: Incorrect – here the jib is blanketed by the mainsail, and producing no power at all.
Fig 2: Correct – here the jib has been poled out on the opposite side where it sets well, unaffected by the airflow on the mainsail.

Gybing, crew movements: Before starting the manoeuvre the helmsman must call out, 'stand by to gybe' to prepare his crew. Then 'gybe-oh' when the boom starts to swing across.

sailing the boat with the wind astern. This is known as running before the wind.

First the helmsman pulls the tiller towards him to bear away and, as the bow turns away from the wind, both main and jib sheets are eased progressively until the boat is pointing down wind and the boom is almost touching the shroud. Look up at the burgee – this will tell you when the wind is coming from astern. As the boat bears away you will find that there is far less heeling moment in the wind and the crew can move inboard to balance the boat.

Another sign that the boat is on a run is that the jib will collapse and refuse to fill. The problem here is that the jib is being over-shadowed by the mainsail and for it to fill this forward sail must be set across on the other side of the boat. This is known as goosewing-ing the jib or sailing goosewinged.

Most dinghies and some cruisers are equipped with a jib stick, or whisker pole as it is sometimes called, which is used to help steady the foresail when set on the opposite side to the main. One end of the pole is clipped to a ring on the mast and the other is attached to the sheet or clew of the sail.

Beginners often think that running before the wind is the easiest part of sailing. It's not, and you will have to steer a steady

course, keeping a wary eye open for any changes in the wind direction if you don't want to be caught out by an unexpected gybe.

Gybing

Gybing is the term used when the boat tacks down wind. An involuntary gybe should be avoided at all costs, but provided that gybing is controlled by the crew and not by the boat it is no more difficult than tacking upwind. It is better for the crew to hand the boom over, rather than allow it to swing freely across, to lessen the risk of an accident or capsize.

When gybing, the helmsman bears away so that the stern passes through the eye of the wind, which gets behind the leech of the mainsail sweeping it across to the other side. The speed at which the sail swings across can worry the beginner but provided that the crew follows a system, little will go wrong.

First the helmsman calls out a warning to his crew, 'stand by to gybe'. Then, once everyone is ready, he gives the instruction 'gybe-oh' and pulls the tiller up towards him so that the boat bears away. It is the crew's job to grasp the kicking strap and pull the boom over as the bow swings round and the helmsman moves across, swapping tiller and mainsheet in his hand as he goes.

Once across, the helmsman checks the boat's turn by pulling the tiller towards him for a moment, and the crew sets the jib, goosewinging it out if the boat is to continue its course running downwind.

With dinghies that rely on crew for balance and stability it is best to gybe all standing – that is to say, allow the mainsail to swing across unchecked as shown in the Mirror. This quick change-over reduces much of the heeling moment and minimizes the chance of capsizing. Most cruisers, however, are much more stable than dinghies and, with a heavier rig to contend with, it is better to sheet in the boom a little at the start of the gybe, releasing it again quickly the moment it crosses over. This limits the swing and lessens the chance of anyone being caught unawares and knocked overboard.

One final point to remember – always gybe the boat when it is travelling at its fastest and not during a lull in the wind or when the boat is 'stopped' at the bottom of a trough in the waves. The pressure on the sails when gybing is much less if the boat is travelling fast, and so the heeling moment is

reduced to a minimum when the sail goes across.

Gybing when the boat has stopped is the most frequent cause of a capsize or broach.

Gybing from a run to a reach: The mainsail is allowed to swing across as the boat alters course and sheeted in when the manoeuvre is complete.

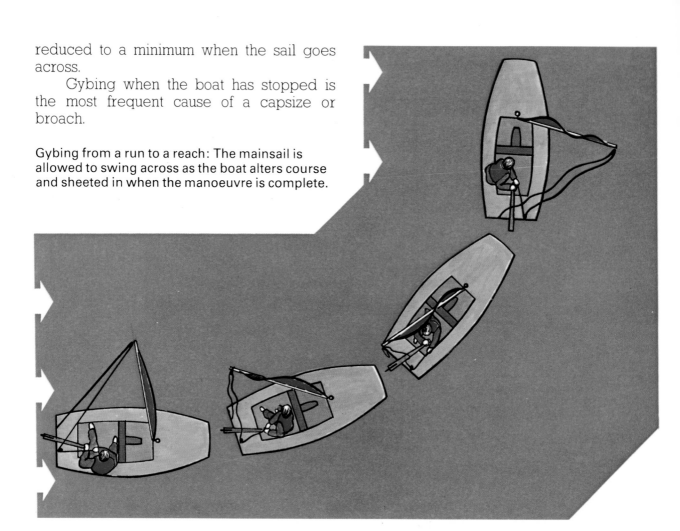

Shifts in the wind direction may require you to alter course or readjust the set of the sails.

Young Mirror dinghy crews enjoying the competition of a close race.

Changing Wind

To start with, beginners often find it difficult to judge the exact wind direction. The wind is rarely steady in either direction or strength and very often the crew will have to alter course or adjust the sails to compensate for this.

The burgee at the top of the mast and telltale lengths of cotton tied to the shrouds will only give an accurate indication of wind direction when the boat is either stationary or sailing downwind. At all other times they indicate only the apparent wind direction, which is the result of the true wind and the forward motion of the boat. Although they act as fair guides, they are not always to be relied upon in very light winds. The best way to judge the true wind direction when sailing is to watch the direction of the surface waves or ripples on the water, keeping an eye open for those dark catspaws – the giveaway sign of an approaching gust.

Gusts often vary in direction and catch the beginner out. If the foresail suddenly starts to flutter it is not always a steering error but may be caused by a shift of the wind from further ahead. This is called a heading or backing shift. If you are beating to windward at the time you will need to bear away; but if the shift happens when you are reaching you need only sheet in the sails and, if you are in a dinghy, lower the centreboard to maintain your course.

If the wind frees – a freeing shift – you will find that the boat will point higher; but should you want to maintain that original course, you merely ease sheets to match the sails to this new wind angle.

Balance

A sailing boat performs best when heeled at an angle of 10 degrees away from the wind, except when the boat is running. Then it should be sailed upright. If the boat is allowed to heel more than 10 degrees the effective area of the keel is reduced and the boat will slip sideways in the water. The boat will also be difficult to steer and the rudder heavy on the helm. With dinghies, the crew has to keep the boat upright by sitting on the weather side, hiking their weight outboard if necessary to counteract the heeling force in the sails. Toe straps are normally fitted on either side of the cockpit for the crew to hook their feet under and balance their weight outboard.

It is up to the forward crew to finely tune this balance and keep the boat upright. The helmsman sits on the weather deck so that he can see forward and can help by leaning out in the heavy winds. However, the forward crew is in a much more manoeuvrable posi-tion and can move his or her weight in and out with the gusts. In light winds it may be necessary for the forward hand to sit well inboard, but always keep a wary eye open for those catspaw signs.

At times the boat will be over-powered by a gust of wind and then it will be the helmsman who has to act quickly by letting out the mainsheet to ease the pressure on the sail. It is only in very strong gusts when a capsize is likely that the crew need release the headsail.

A cruiser has a heavy keel to keep it upright, but in strong winds it still helps to have the crew sitting on the weather side. But it is just as important to sail the boat upright as it is with a dinghy, and if the boat is continually overpressed then the crew will either have to take in a reef or change to smaller sails.

Below left: Some boats like this Mini sail have a sliding seat to aid sitting out, but in the Finn Olympic dinghy (*below*) the helmsman, supported only by toe straps, must hike out hard to keep the boat level.
Opposite: In some two-man boats like this Olympic 470, the crewman can make use of a trapeze to increase the leverage on the rig.

Seamanship

Good seamanship is a blend of experience and common sense. It means bringing a boat neatly to a halt within nudging distance of a mooring buoy, then sailing off again through a crowded anchorage. It means bringing the boat alongside a busy harbour wall without causing strife or worry to other nearby crews, and ultimately it could mean rescuing another yacht in distress in strong winds and heavy seas. It takes time, practice and patience to learn to sail but, once you are proficient, each well executed manoeuvre brings with it a deep sense of satisfaction as a reward.

Leaving a Mooring

For dinghy sailors, leaving a mooring is a fairly simple manoeuvre since a light boat with little draught will lie head to wind once the sails are hoisted, whichever way the tide is running, in anything but the faintest of breezes.

Cruisers, however, with their deeper draught, are affected much more by the current and unless both wind and water are coming from the same direction, a different technique is required.

Let's start by dealing with dinghies and cruisers that are lying head to wind (Fig 1). The first job is to hoist the sails – but check that the sheets are free, otherwise the boat will start to sail around the mooring. Check that the tiller is free and the centreplate, if there is one, is down. Once everything is shipshape, one crew member can prepare to release the mooring line. When this is free to be dropped, the headsail is backed to the opposite side to the way that you want to leave the mooring so that it pushes the bow round.

Once the mainsail starts to fill, the skipper calls, 'let go' and the crew releases the mooring warp. The headsail is brought across, sheeted in on the correct side, and you're away!

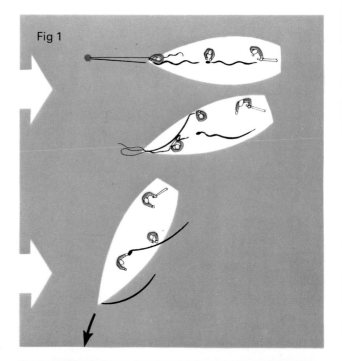

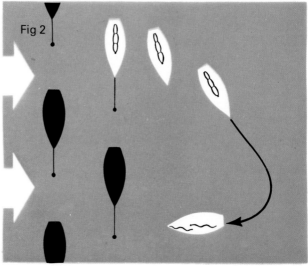

Fig 1: Leaving a mooring when head to wind.
Fig 2: Leaving a mooring with wind abeam.
Fig 3: Returning to a mooring, head to wind.
Fig 4: Returning to a mooring with wind abeam.
Fig 5: Returning to a mooring, downwind.

When, on the other hand, the current is running across or against the direction of the wind and the boat will not lie head-to, it is best to leave the mainsail bent on the boom ready for hoisting, and sail off the mooring under headsail alone. The boat can then be turned head to wind in a clear stretch of water ready for the mainsail to be hoisted (Fig 2).

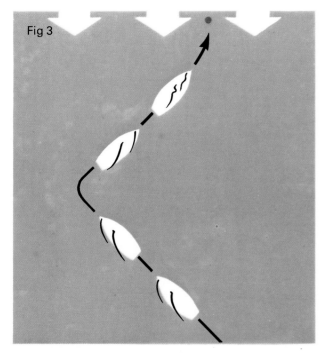

Fig 3

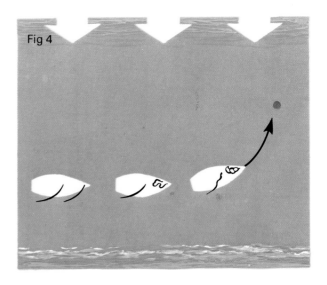

Fig 4

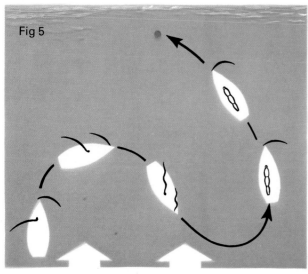

Fig 5

However, in a busy anchorage where there will be little room to manoeuvre, it would certainly be prudent to leave the mooring under power and hoist the sails in a less crowded area.

Returning to a Mooring

This is a manoeuvre that certainly needs plenty of practice, whatever size boat you sail. The skipper has to learn how much way his boat will carry once sheets have been eased and gauge its turning circle, as well as judging the effect of the tide. No set of conditions ever seems the same but experience will teach you to judge each occasion individually and accurately.

The dinghy helmsman has fewer problems to cope with, since being light his boat will not carry much way. The best approach is to sail close hauled up to the mooring, easing sheets as you near the buoy to slow down, then turn up head to wind to bring the boat to a halt right by the mark (Fig 3).

The secret is to keep just enough way on the boat so that it stops right by the buoy. Make the approach too fast and the crew may find it difficult or even impossible to hang on to the buoy; make the approach too slow and the boat will lose way before the buoy comes within reach. If you miss the buoy, sheet in the sails to get some way on the boat again, sail back down wind, tack, and have another go.

Once the mooring warp has been grasped, pulled through the fairlead and made fast on the cleat, the forward hand must always shout back to the crew in the cockpit, 'all secure' and, on that call, sails have to be lowered immediately, otherwise the boat will start to sail all round the mooring.

Some moorings are not always approachable from down wind and it is necessary to sail up on a reach – the fastest point of sailing. The simplest way to reduce speed is to lower the foresail in plenty of time, then ease the mainsheet right out to take off all way on the boat as you near the mark (Fig 4). Approaching a mark down wind is probably the hardest manoeuvre to

judge. The first thing to do is turn head to wind well before the mark and lower the mainsail, then continue under headsail alone. This is dropped when you judge that the boat has enough way on to reach the buoy. The windage on a mast is quite considerable – certainly enough to drive the boat along but if you find that the sails were lowered too early, part hoist the headsail once more and this will give you sufficient power to sail on to the mark (Fig 5).

Leaving the Shore

When the wind is blowing onshore the boat has to be turned head to wind with the bows facing out to sea. It will probably be easier to hoist the sails once the boat is afloat.

The man at the bow has to walk the dinghy out into deep enough water for the centreplate and rudder to be lowered slightly, before the bow is pushed off the wind and he clambers aboard. Both rudder blade and centreboard will have to be lowered gradually as the boat sails into deeper water, otherwise the wind will force the boat to slip sideways without making forward progress at all.

When the wind is blowing offshore, the boat is pushed out from the beach, stern first,

With the wind blowing onshore, the crew must wade out with the boat until the water is deep enough to put the rudder down.

so that the sails remain set head to wind. Then whilst one crew member steadies the bow, the helmsman and others clamber aboard. When everything is shipshape, the man at the bow pushes the head round so that the sails fill and climbs aboard himself as the boat starts to make way. Keep the sheets well eased until the boat is out into deeper water and the rudder blade can be pushed right down.

Returning to Shore

It is easiest to return to a windward shore and the same procedure is used as that of picking up a mooring. Sail inshore on a tack, easing the sheets, and turn the boat head to wind to lose way just before it grounds. At the same time the centreboard and rudder will need to be raised gradually as you near the shore to stop them grounding. But don't pull them up too early, otherwise the boat will make more leeway than headway. If there are any waves the crew will have to jump out quickly to steady the boat when it grounds.

Sailing on to a lee shore can be a

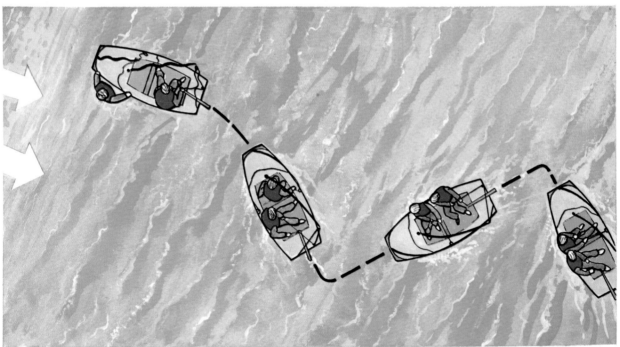

Top: When the wind is blowing offshore, the boat must be pushed out stern first.

Above: Returning to a windward shore the crew jump out to steady the boat before she grounds.

hazardous operation, especially in windy conditions. You will find it best to drop the sails early and either paddle your way ashore or sail it under jib alone. As soon as the crew can touch bottom they should jump out and spin the boat round to face the waves, otherwise they may break over the stern and swamp the boat.

Beaching a Dinghy

If you are going ashore for a short stay or picnic, always spare a thought for the tide. A

31

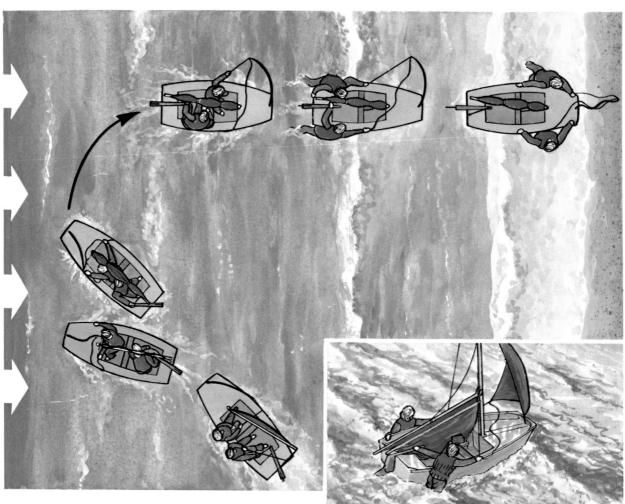

Returning to a lee shore it is often easiest to drop the mainsail early and sail in under jib alone.

light boat can be carried up the beach but heavier craft will need to be anchored. When the tide is on the ebb the small dinghy will not have to be carried very far but an anchored boat will need to be secured on a long warp to ensure that it doesn't dry out later on. The anchor's warp requires plenty of scope – the longer it is the better it will hold – but always check that the anchor is well stamped in before leaving.

If the dinghy is carried up the beach it should still be secured with a line ashore, just in case the tide comes up higher than you thought it would.

Dropping Anchor

An anchor will only hold properly in the sea bed if the pull from the warp is parallel to the ground, and all require at least 2 fathoms (4 m or 12 ft) of chain linking between warp and anchor to weight the stock down. The amount of warp let out is also critical. If there is too little scope, the tugging movements from the boat riding the waves will lift the chain off the bottom, with the result that the anchor will break out and drag. As a rule of thumb, the length of warp paid out should approximately be four or five times the depth of water at high tide.

The best way to check whether the boat is dragging is to sight two or more land marks and line them up with the shore, then check their positions again five minutes later. The size of anchor is also important and the general guide given below matches boat length with the weight of anchor (Danforth and C.Q.R. types) required.

Overall length	Anchor size
Under 12 ft	5 lb
12 ft–15 ft	10 lb
16 ft–20 ft	12 lb
21 ft–27 ft	17 lb
28 ft–40 ft	30 lb
41 ft–50 ft	43 lb

Always tie the anchor warp off on the central bollard on the foredeck (this is normally the strongest fitting aboard) and lead the warp through a fairlead on the bow to stop it chafing. As a safety measure, especially when picking up an existing mooring, it is as well to tie a second line, securing the warp to the cleat so that it cannot come free of its own accord.

Making Fast Alongside

So many beginners fail to remember the tide when tying up alongside a wall or jetty. However, the sight of your boat swinging perilously from bollards like a trussed turkey with the waters several feet below will be a lesson never forgotten.

The correct way to tie up alongside is shown overleaf and generally speaking one should allow sufficient scope on the warps to cover three times the rise and fall of tide at low water. The warps will have to be adjusted as the tide rises. The head and stern warps take most of the loadings and the springs hold the boat neatly alongside, whichever way the water flows.

A yacht which is likely to take the ground as the tide recedes must always be 'watched' down to ensure that it settles correctly and that there has been sufficient

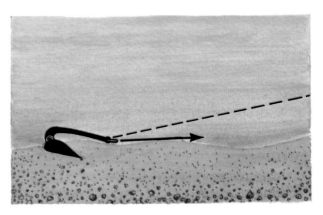

Anchors will require at least two fathoms of chain to weight the stock down on the seabed, and usually the warp paid out should be four to five times the depth of water at high tide.

scope given to the warps.

The danger is that the boat may lean out from the wall. The answer is to move enough weight around below or even bring some ballast up on deck to give the yacht a 5–10 degree list inwards before she settles on the ground.

Don't forget to hang the fenders over the side before coming alongside – just one accidental scrape can cause hundreds of pounds worth of damage. But remember to pull them in when you set sail again. Fenders hanging over the side not only look untidy, they're a sure sign that beginners are aboard!

Lying Hove-to

There will be times when you want to stop the boat sailing for short periods without dropping anchor. This is a manoeuvre known as *lying hove-to* and can be done in any but the strongest of winds.

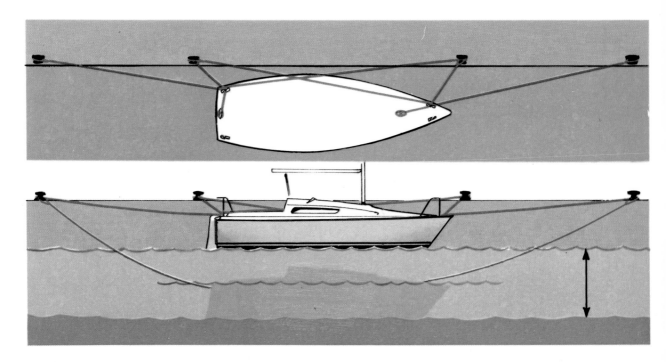

When tying up allow scope on the warps to cover three times the rise and fall of the tide.

The easiest way is to sheet the headsail in hard on one tack, then go about, leaving the sail cleated but releasing the mainsheet once the foresail is backwinded. However, where sea-room is limited or other boats are nearby, it is best to stay on the same tack and merely back the jib across to the other side. To counteract the pressure on the headsail from pushing the bow round, the tiller has to be held or tied down on the opposite side. Remember when lying hove-to, to keep an eye open on the boat's sideways drift.

Reefing

Sailors don't only reduce sail in strong winds for the obvious safety reasons – it can improve the performance of the boat as well. Boats, regardless of size, are designed to be sailed at a maximum heel of approximately 10 degrees. Pressed any further and the keels or centreboards start to lose their efficiency and the boat slips sideways through the water.

When leaving a mooring, only experience will tell you exactly which sails are right for the strength of wind and sea conditions

and, to start with, it is always best to err on the conservative side. Most cruisers will carry a number of different-sized headsails and it is normally a simple matter to lower one, replacing it with a smaller jib. However, the position of the sheet blocks may have to be moved to suit the different sails. Correct sheeting angle is very important and the line of the sheet should approximately bisect the clew of the sail, as the illustration shows, to give the same tension to both foot and leech of the sail. Reefing the mainsail on a cruiser is a little more complex and varies according to the system fitted.

Roller reefing (Fig 6)
As the name implies, the sail is gathered in by rolling it around the boom. The main halyard is uncleated and paid out slowly as the boom is revolved with its handle, wrapping the sail around it. The secret to a neat reef is to smooth all the creases out towards the leech and remove the battens as the pockets approach the boom.

Slab reefing (Fig 7)
Slab reefing is one of the quickest methods of

Lying hove-to is one way to stop the boat sailing without dropping anchor. The mainsail is let free, the jib pulled across to the weather side, the tiller held down and the centreboard half-raised.

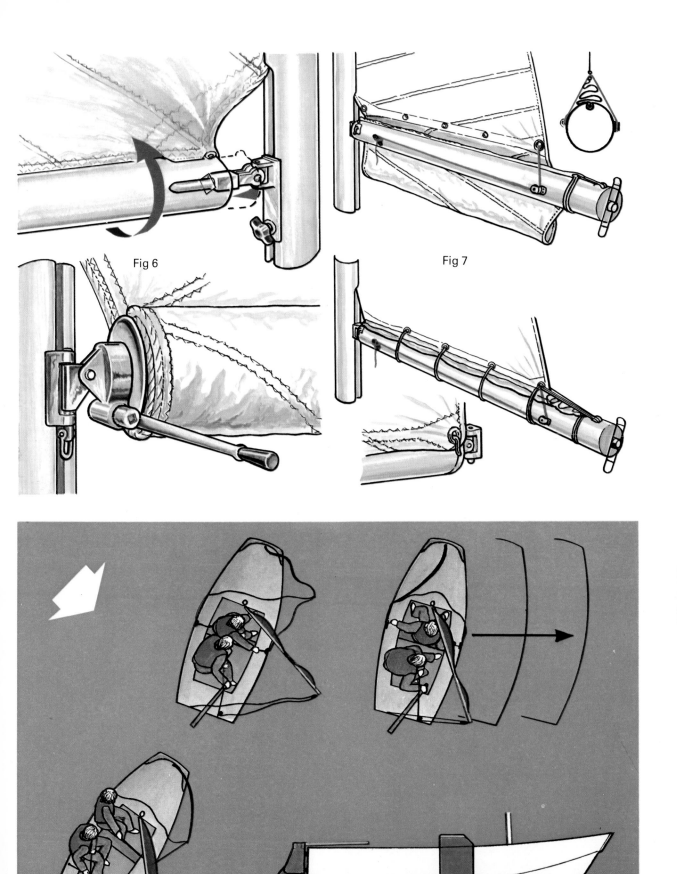

Fig 6

Fig 7

Fig 8

Fig 9

Fig 10

Fig 11

Fig 12

reducing the area of the mainsail and does less harm to the sail than roller reefing, where the material tends to be pulled out of shape as it is rolled around the boom. Reefing lines are passed through cringles in the leech of the mainsail and one end is tied to the boom while the other is passed through a block on the opposite side and run forward to a cleat. These lines should always be rigged when the sail is hoisted so that it is ready to be reefed at any time. The sail area is reduced by uncleating the halyard and lowering the sail so that the cringle, fitted in the luff of the sail on the same parallel line to the leech cringle, can be attached to a hook fitted on the forward end of the boom. At the same time the reefing line attached to the cringle in the leech is tightened so that the cringle lies on the boom and is then cleated. The loose sail can now be folded inside itself and lashed to the boom using short lines tied through the smaller cringles in the middle of the sail.

Capsize and Recovery

Even the best dinghy sailors capsize from time to time and, like horse riders, they are reckoned to lack experience until their first fall.

A successful recovery from a capsize is often the turning point in gaining self confidence afloat. A deliberate capsize in sheltered waters should be part of every sailor's training and the best way to learn is to memorize and practise this standard routine.

1. After a capsize never swim away from the boat, even if you wish to retrieve loose gear – wind and currents can work together to push the boat away faster than you can swim back (Fig 8).

2. One crewman should climb on to the centreboard whilst the others stay in the vicinity of the bow or stern, holding on lightly to keep the dinghy head to wind during this recovery exercise (Fig 9).

3. The crewman balancing on the board now grabs the nearest jib sheet, pulling it

This Mirror crew is pulling on the wrong end of the jib sheet (see Fig 3) and with the wind filling the sail, this can stop the boat from coming upright. The second crew is also hindering recovery by attempting to climb aboard before the boat is upright. She should be holding on to the bow (or stern) lightly to keep the boat head to wind.

through the fairlead until the knot comes up against it so that the sail remains free (Fig 10).

4. He then leans on the sheet to pull the mast and sails clear of the water.

5. The boat will automatically pivot round in the water until it is pointing head to wind, provided that the other crew are not holding on tightly and acting as a sea anchor. It will hasten matters if they help to push the bow round into the wind.

6. Once facing the wind, the boat will suddenly come upright and the man on the centreboard will have to clamber quickly in over the side and release any sheets that are cleated, otherwise the boat is likely to roll right over on top of him (Fig 11).

7. Those still in the water can now climb back on board over the stern where their weight will make little difference to trim.

8. The water is bailed out and once sheets and loose gear have been sorted, the boat can be sailed away (Fig 12).

If the crew are thrown into the sail or stand on the mast after a capsize, some boats have a tendency to turn turtle. In such cases the crew must stand on the gunwale and lean back on the centreboard to bring the dinghy back to a horizontal attitude before starting the standard routine.

Spinnakers

The Spinnaker is a subject best left until last because crews need to have a good appreciation of how a boat sails before attempting to set this off-wind sail. It is not the simplest of tasks to perform, and if things go wrong you can find yourself in considerable difficulty.

Pick a day when the wind is blowing a steady force 2–3 and invite an experienced hand to come along and help. This is a sail that can easily get out of control if mistakes are made during hoisting or setting, so you should always go cautiously when learning. The illustrations below show the air flow around a spinnaker when set on both a run and reach. Sailing straight down wind (Fig 1), the sail merely catches the air from astern which helps to push the boat along. When the sail is set on a reach, however, as in the second picture (Fig 2), the spinnaker has to be trimmed, just like the other sails, so that the airflow passes across its surface. It is in this position that the sail generates most power.

Spinnakers bring both fun and colour to cruising but it is best to practise on a calm day first, otherwise there could be trouble.

Setting a Spinnaker

The diagrams show how a spinnaker is set on a dinghy and the heavier arrangement that is required on small cruisers like our Salty Dog. The main point to remember is that the spinnaker and all its gear has to be set outside everything – including the life lines on a cruiser. The spinnaker pole is always set on the windward side and two lines control the spinnaker from the lower corners of the sail.

The guy is the term used for the control line which is attached to the clew on the windward side of the sail and runs through the end of the spinnaker pole, while the sheet is attached to and controls the leeward

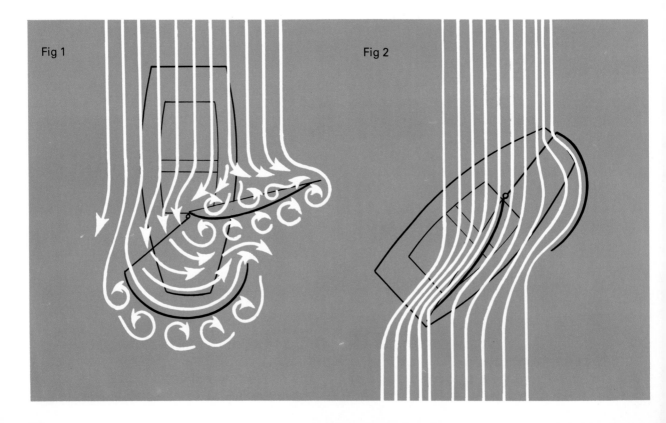

Fig 1

Fig 2

clew. When the boat is sailing on the opposite gybe then the two spinnaker control lines exchange both their functions and descriptions.

The spinnaker is hoisted by a halyard which is attached to the head of the sail. On dinghies, the spinnaker pole is connected to the mast with a quick release clip clamping over an eye which is attached to the spar. In the case of most cruisers the pole is fitted into a cup linked to a slider on the mast, and at the outboard end is supported both by uphaul and downhaul control lines.

On dinghies, however, the downhaul and lift usually consist of a single line carrying a series of stopper knots along its length. These lock into a cleat mid-way along the pole to control its setting.

1 Spinnaker crane
2 Inglefield clips and swivel
3 Halyard
4 Headboard
5 Elastic uphaul
6 Spinnaker boom
7 Tack
8 Tack ring
9 Guy clip
10 Cleat
11 Eye plate
12 Downhaul
13 Stop knob
14 Guy
15 Halyard Sheave
16 Sheet
17 Snatch lead
18 Downhaul cleat
19 Boom stowage clip

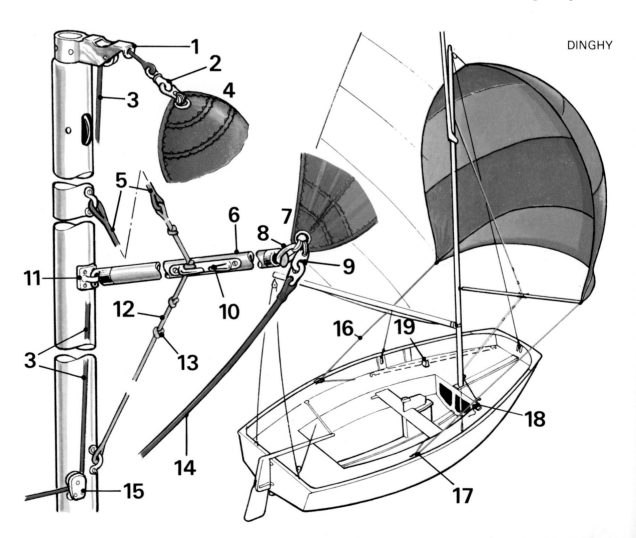

DINGHY

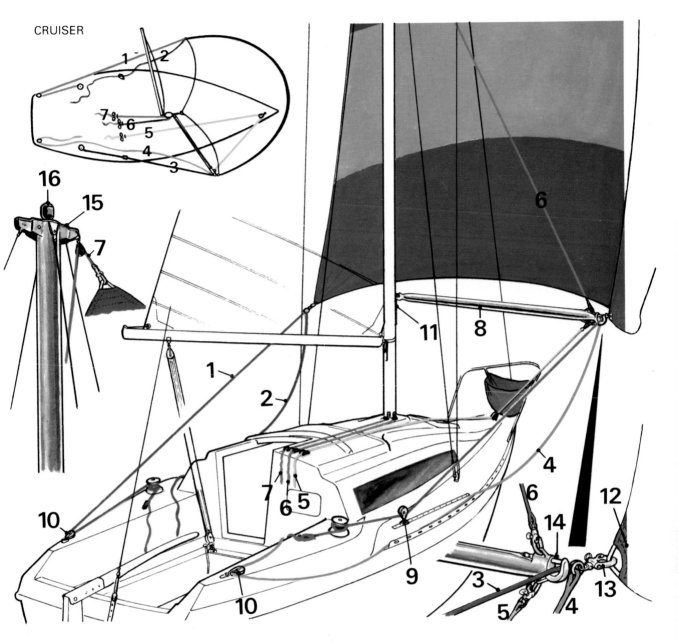

1 Sheet
2 Lazy sheet
3 Guy
4 Lazy guy
5 Foreguy
6 Pole lift
7 Halyard
8 Spinnaker pole
9 Guy lead block and track
10 Sheet block
11 Track and sliding eye
12 Clew
13 Snap shackle
14 Release plunger
15 Masthead crane
16 Bi-colour navigation light

Packing a Spinnaker

Packing a spinnaker correctly is very important in order to ensure that the sail is not hoisted with a twist in it. On a cruiser the sail is often stowed in a spinnaker turtle – a special bag with a wide neck supported with wire which is attached inside the pulpit rail prior to hoisting. In dinghies without spinnaker chutes, the sail is stowed in one of two bags sited on either side of the mast, or, as in the case of our Mirror, it may be stowed in an open compartment situated under the foredeck.

When packing the spinnaker the three corners must be arranged so that they finish up at the top, ready for the halyard, sheet and guy to be attached.

The bottom starboard corner of the spinnaker is identified by the green webbing stitched along its edge, whilst the port clew is marked with red and the head has corresponding green and red webbing on either side of the apex.

Packing the sail, it is often easier if two people work together, each taking a clew and folding the sail into a series of flakes along the leeches which are held in the hand. Once this operation is completed, one of the crew then takes over holding both folded leeches in his hand whilst the other stuffs the remainder of the sail into the bag, placing the folded parts in last with the clews and head patches uppermost.

Where there is a choice of stowage bags in a dinghy, think which gybe the boat will be sailing on when the spinnaker is first required and stow the sail on the leeward side, which is always the easiest position to hoist from. Finally the halyard, sheet and guy are attached to their respective corners of the sail and are cleated in place. Always remember to double check that the lines run outside everything.

Hoisting the spinnaker on a run.

With large spinnakers it can often simplify handling if the sail is 'stopped' prior to hoisting with light rubber bands. Then instead of flaking the leeches out the sail is passed head first through a bottomless plastic bucket with sufficient rubber bands slipped over it to stop the sail at three foot intervals. As one person holds the head, the two clews are pulled taut to ensure that there are no twists, and the bucket is passed along from one end of the sail to the other while the bands are peeled off at three foot intervals. The sail can now be hoisted without fear of it blowing out until the sheet and guy are pulled to break the stops.

Hoisting the Spinnaker

It is always both easier and safer to hoist the spinnaker on the leeward side so that the sail is blanketed by the mainsail as it goes up. If this is done it will be less likely to fill with wind before you are ready for it, and will be far more easily controlled.

Hoisting on a run

When hoisting the spinnaker on a run, most dinghies will be stable enough for the helmsman to straddle the tiller and steer with his knees. This will leave his hands free to haul on the halyard, which should be led back to a

cleat that is within easy reach. As the helmsman pulls rapidly on the halyard, the crew has to haul on the guy to pull the weather clew round the forestay. The crew then picks up the spinnaker pole and attaching the outboard end of it to the guy, pushes it out until it runs up against the clew of the sail.

The uphaul/downhaul control line should then be attached to its cleat mid-way along the spinnaker pole, which is then clipped into its position on the mast.

Once the helmsman has hoisted the spinnaker and cleated off the halyard, he helps to control the sail by taking the sheet and guy in either hand, pulling in the slack and getting the sail to pull as soon as the pole is rigged. Taking up a position on the weather side of the boat so that he can have a good view of the sail, the crew then takes over the control lines from the helmsman, cleating the guy with the pole set at 90° to the apparent wind, and adjusting the sheet to a point where the luff of the sail is about to collapse. The helmsman meanwhile sits on the leeward side of the boat in order to balance the crew weight.

On a cruiser, the same operation takes place except that the work is shared amongst more people. The helmsman can therefore concentrate on steering a steady course, while another crew member hoists the spinnaker, the foredeck hand rigs the pole, and other crew in the cockpit take care of the sheet and guy and pole downhaul.

Hoisting on a Reach
Hoisting the spinnaker on a reach can be a much more difficult operation to control if the sail is not pulled up and set promptly. This is because with the boat sailing across the wind, the sail may fill before the crew is ready and wrap itself around the rigging.

In a dinghy the centreboard should be half raised in the normal manner for reaching, and the pole rigged on the mast with the guy running through the end fitting, before any thought is given to hoisting the sail. Once this preparatory operation is completed the helmsman, sitting on the windward side this time to keep the boat balanced, reaches over to hoist the sail. At the same time the crew pulls in on the guy to bring the clew round the forestay and up against the pole, which again has to be set at an angle of 90° to the apparent wind. For the moment there is no need to worry about the sheet since the spinnaker will flap harmlessly to leeward until both halyard and guy are cleated off in their correct positions. Only when both helmsman and crew are ready to balance the boat should the sheet be pulled in to get the spinnaker pulling.

On a cruiser the same routine applies, though with more hands on deck life will be

made a little easier. Again, the helmsman can concentrate on steering while the foredeck hand sets the pole and others hoist and trim the sail from the cockpit. When reaching, it is sometimes easier to pull the spinnaker up behind the headsail – this helps blanket the wind during the hoist. However the genoa will have to be lowered once the spinnaker is setting if this offwind sail is to work efficiently.

Spinnaker Trimming

Basic spinnaker trimming is the same on any size of boat and is a compromize between exposing the maximum area of sail to the wind while simultaneously encouraging the

Hoisting the spinnaker on a reach.

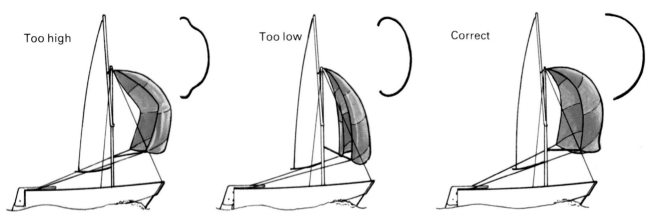

Too high   Too low   Correct

Spinnaker pole height.

air to flow across it.

When sailing straight down the wind the air flow merely pushes on the sail and since little cross-flow is achieved it is important to expose the maximum area of cloth to the wind. In light winds with the mainsail boomed right out on one side, the spinnaker can be pulled round to a point almost 90° to the centreline. However it should not be pulled round so far in strong winds when the slot between spinnaker and mainsail has to be opened more in order to exhaust the air.

The crew, who should hold the sheet at all times, has to learn to play the sail so that the luff of the spinnaker is always on the point of breaking or curling inwards. Keeping his eye on the luff he has to 'tweak' the sheet in when it starts to curl; then let it out again slowly until the sail takes up the correct shape, to a point where the luff is starting to collapse again. When experienced, a good crew constantly tweaking and easing the sheet will be able to keep the spinnaker on the point of breaking all the time.

Changing Course

When changing from a run to a reach the pole angle has to be altered so that it remains at 90° to the apparent wind angle. As the pole is eased forward on the guy the sheet has to be pulled in to keep the luff of the spinnaker on the point of collapse.

On a cruiser, where the uphaul and downhaul is attached to the end of the spinnaker pole, the downhaul will have to be adjusted to suit the new angle, otherwise the pole will tend to sky when swung forward.

Height of Pole

The height of the pole also has a direct bearing on the set of the spinnaker. Ideally the two clews should always be level and the cross section of the sail set in an even curve. If the pole is set too high then the luff and leech will tend to collapse forward and valuable power will be lost. Remember though that this is sometimes no bad thing in heavy winds when the boat may be overpressed. If the pole is set too low then the clews will not remain level, the leeches will be drawn too taut and the luff will want to curl in too early.

Gybing the Spinnaker

Ideally, not a drop of wind should be lost when gybing the spinnaker from one side to another and the sail should continue pulling throughout the manoeuvre. When gybing in dinghies and on some small cruisers it is easiest to 'end-for-end' the pole, but on larger cruisers with heavier equipment and larger sail areas it is often better to use the 'dip-pole' method.

In dinghies, the boat is brought onto a dead run and the helmsman, steering with the tiller between his knees, takes over control of the sheet and guy. These should be adjusted so that they are at the same length, with the pole angled at 45° to the centreline. The crew now moves forward on the leeward side to unclip the pole and, as the main

Crew work when gybing on a run.

boom swings over, he then pulls the pole across to clip it onto the new guy. Once it is attached the crew can then release the opposite end of the pole from the new sheet and clip this to the mast. With this completed the helmsman then hands back the sheet and guy and both can take up their working positions once more.

Dip-Pole Gybe

With this method, the pole is swung forward and the guy released from its outboard end as the main boom gybes across. Then the downhaul is released to allow the tip of the pole to sweep the deck and pass inside the forestay, ready to be re-hoisted to its correct height and attached to the new guy.

Lowering the Spinnaker

It is easiest if you always lower the sail on the

leeward side where it is blanketed by the mainsail. In a dinghy the sheet is cleated and the crew then moves forward to release the pole from both mast and guy before stowing it. He then grasps the sheet and gathers in the foot of the sail so that the leeches are pulled down together. At the same time the helmsman lowers the halyard keeping pace with the crew who stows the sail back in its container, taking care not to twist the leeches. Once the sail is safely away the crew then cleats the halyard and control lines so that they cannot drag it out again. The important point is that the halyard should not be played out faster than the sail is being gathered in; otherwise the spinnaker can drop into the water.

On larger boats it is not easy to pull the sail down in this manner; instead, the fore-deck hand goes forward to release the snap-shackle which holds guy to clew so that the sail streams aft on the sheet. Then as the halyard is released, the cockpit crew gathers in the sail under the main boom, passing it down through the hatch ready for re-packing in its turtle bag.

Problems with Spinnakers

One of the most common problems when hoisting the spinnaker is the hour-glass twist. It is caused either through a slow hoist which allows the sail to flog, twisting itself around, or by careless packing. To avoid this happening, you should always hoist the sail quickly and haul in the loose sheet and guy to keep the leeches apart. Once the sail is twisted however, the best answer is to lower the sail and unravel the twists by hand before hoisting it back up, taking in the slack this time on both sheet and guy to keep the leeches apart.

A violent broach in a dinghy invariably leads to a capsize, or, in the case of a cruiser, leaves the yacht lying on its beam ends with

Lowering the spinnaker.

Fig 3

Fig 4

Fig 5

Fig 6

Fig 7

Problems with spinnakers: Set on a reach the spinnaker can pose many problems for the crew. If the guy and sheet fairlead block are set in the wrong position on the gunnel the sheet can sometimes ride over the end of the main boom (Fig 3). If it is not possible to move the blocks to a better position further forward one answer is to attach barber-haulers (Fig 4). These are short

control lines with a ring or block attached to the outboard end through which the sheet runs, and, cleated on the deck, can be tensioned to lower the clew height of the spinnaker.
Fig 5: Always remember to tie figure of eight knots in the end of both the spinnaker sheet and guy, otherwise the sail is bound to run free.
Fig 6: Never hoist the spinnaker before first

sails flogging. It is most likely to occur on a close reach where the excessive sideways force generated in the sail causes the boat to heel over. This lifts the rudder partially out of the water, decreasing the helmsman's ability to steer. In this uncontrolled state the boat then pivots on its lee side, swinging round up into the wind. To prevent this from occurring the boat has to be sailed upright, and the spinnaker sheet eased off smartly the moment she starts to heel.

A weather roll in a dinghy also often leads to a capsize, while in keel boats this sickening motion can develop into a violent broach. The rolling is the result of a side force on the rig when the spinnaker is set too far round the windward side.

The simplest way to correct this imbalance is to haul in quickly on the sheet to pull the sail round; then, when the boat is stable again, release the guy, allowing the pole to swing forward at 90° to the apparent wind.

setting the pole with the guy attached.
Fig 7: If the spinnaker is hoisted before the guy is tensioned to pull the clew up against the end of the spinnaker pole, the sail is likely to set inside the foretriangle which often leads to a capsize.
Fig 8: The classic hour-glass twist, caused either through a slow hoist or careless packing.
Fig 9: If the spinnaker is set too far round the boat will start to roll. The answer is to pull in smartly on the sheet or reset the guy.

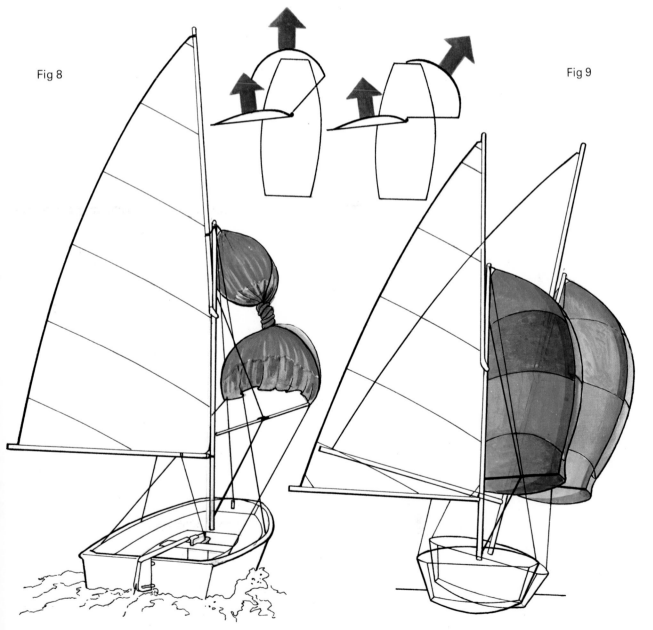

Fig 8

Fig 9

Knots

Coming to terms

I well remember an old salt chastizing me during my early days of sail after I had asked him to pass up a rope.

'There's only one rope aboard a boat,' he told me, 'and that's for beginners to hang themselves by.'

Every rope has a name and must be called by it. There are a great many terms to learn but it is the only way to make yourself understood when calling for a sail to be pulled in or an anchor raised. Similarly, learning about knots is one of the first lessons in seamanship – and not just for one member of the crew. If every one on board uses the same knots to tie off halyards, sheets and warps, many a panic will be averted. If sails have to be lowered and a warp found in a hurry when the boat refuses to stop for the harbour wall ahead, the crew will only know how to unfurl those ropes quickly if they also know how they were coiled in the first place.

With the advent of synthetic rope and stainless steel wire much of the traditional ropework has been lost, but there are still a number of basic knots and splices that are in regular use afloat. It's as well to have a small bag of tools to hand – a sharp knife, splicing fid, sewing palm, pliers and a shackle key, together with a sail-cloth needle and Terylene thread, will simplify life considerably.

Figure of eight knot

This is the knot most of us learn first when crewing. It is the traditional stopper knot tied into the end of sheets and halyards to save the tails running out through blocks or cleats. It is a knot that never jams, however much pressure is applied, and can be untied with a twist of the thumb.

Bowline

The bowline is the best knot to form a fixed loop in the end of rope. It never slips or jams and even after severe tension it is simple to loosen it. To form the knot, a loop is made in the rope and the tail is then threaded up through, round behind the standing part, and pulled tight once it has been laced back through the loop again. An association of ideas is always a good way to remember things. For a bowline think of the tail of the rope as a rabbit that comes up out of its hole, goes round the tree and then back down the hole again.

Reef knot

This is one of the oldest methods of joining two lengths of cord together, and is used for knotting sail ties. It should never be used where the two cords are of different sizes or materials since it is likely to jam and be impossible to untie.

Never mistake it for the Granny knot which is tied the opposite way and is totally unreliable. The reef knot is made by tying two overhand knots; one a cross-over from left to right, the other from right to left. It is best remembered with the phrase, 'left over right, right over left'.

Sheet bend

This is the hitch that fishermen use for tying

Fig 1: Figure of eight knot.
Fig 2: Bowline knot.
Fig 3: Reef knot.

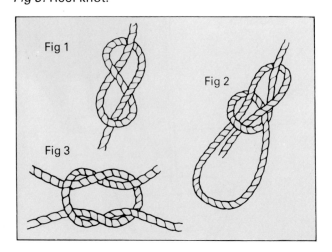

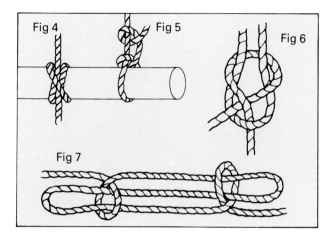

Fig 4: Clove hitch.
Fig 5: Round turn and two half hitches.
Fig 6: Sheet bend.
Fig 7: Sheep shank.

their nets, but its most common use aboard is for knotting ropes of different thicknesses and materials together. It is formed by making a bight in one rope and tying a half hitch with the other, having passed the tail through the centre of the bight first.

Clove hitch

This is the hitch that is used to tie a line to a spar. It is also frequently used to secure fender lines to lifelines or stanchions, or to tie temporary ratlines to the shrouds, which is why it is sometimes known as the 'ratline hitch.' It can be made in one of two ways; either by passing the end around, first over and then under itself, or by dropping two turns over a post.

Round turn and two half hitches

This is a knot that has plenty of uses aboard; for example, tying a mooring warp to a ring or a rope round a spar. It is very simple to tie – all you have to do is pass the rope round twice and add two half hitches to the standing part.

Sheep shank

You may often need to shorten a rope when it is not possible to take up the slack at one end. The sheep shank is just the knot for the job. The rope is laid out or held in two bights, and a half hitch is formed at each end of the tail. This is a good knot to remember when you need to shorten a mooring warp.

Coiling rope

There is nothing worse than finding a warp or halyard wrapped up in a tangled mess. Invariably, these ropes need to be run free in a hurry and so must always be coiled ready for a quick release. Most stranded rope is laid right handed. To stop it from kinking, make up the coil in a clockwise manner, so that any rogue twists or turns are chased down the rope. The best way to tidy up the loose ends around the mast is to hang the coiled halyards on their cleats, pulling the first loop through the middle of the coil, and giving it a twist before hooking it up on the horn. Warps and spare sheets can be coiled in the same way, and then secured with a buntline hitch.

Making fast on a cleat

Securing ropes onto a cleat is one job that all crew must do correctly, otherwise a knife will be needed to sort out the resulting tangle. A full turn must be taken around the cleat, then as many figure of eight turns as

Fig 8: Coiling rope.
Fig 9: Coil of rope secured with a buntline hitch.
Fig 10: Coil of rope stowed on its cleat by pulling first loop through the middle and giving it a twist before hooking on the horn.

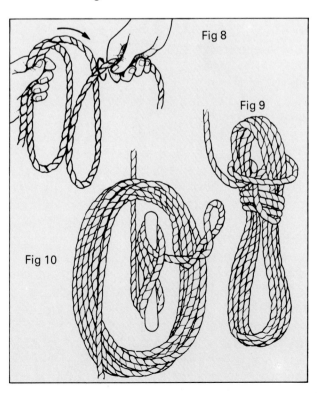

Making fast onto a cleat using a full turn and figures of eight.

possible are added before finishing off with a half hitch. Sheets that are for ever being adjusted to suit a skipper's whim will hold with the figure of eight turns alone. The final half hitch takes time to undo and is a finishing knot for rope that is to be left untended.

Back splice

One of the many advantages that synthetic rope has over its natural counterpart is that the ends can be fused with a hot knife blade to prevent the strands unravelling. (If a hot knife is not available, a flame will do the job almost as well.)

When you are cutting synthetic rope, it is best to bind the point with a layer of plastic tape. The rope can then be cut, leaving the tape holding the strand ends together as a temporary measure until heat is applied. Sharp edges left by the hot knife blade can be removed by running wet fingers over the ends while they cool.

One of the neatest ways to stop natural rope from fraying is to splice the ends. The three strand back splice is begun with a crown knot. Unravel the final 15 cm (6 in) of rope to separate the strands. The crown knot is formed by looping strand B over to the opposite side of the rope, then doing the same with strand A. Strand C is then passed around A and laced through the loop made by B. The knot is drawn tight by pulling at each strand a little at a time. Once firm, the loose ends are tucked under every second strand in the rope, each end being given a tuck in turn and pulled tight. A minimum of four tucks should be made before the ends

are cut off, but the splice can be tapered into the rope if the loose strands are thinned with a sharp knife before the final tuck is made.

Whipping

One of the problems with an end splice is that it increases the circumference of the rope. Where sheets or halyards are led through a block it is sometimes preferable to whip the end with Terylene twine. Whipping should always run against the lay of the rope, and life is made much easier by working towards the tail.

Our illustration shows the first moves you make, with the end of the twine placed short of the rope tail and the first whipping turns made. The total length of whipping should equal a little over the rope's diameter, and when this is achieved, with each turn drawn as tight as possible, the end of the twine is laid back down the whipping and three further turns are wound round. Then the final turn is drawn tight and the ends cut off.

Whipping three-strand rope.

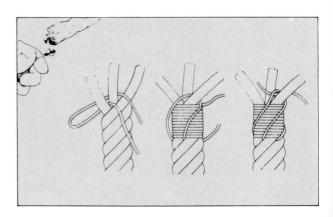

Three strand splice

A well-made three strand short splice is one of the strongest methods of uniting two ropes. Unravel the last 15 cm (6 in) of each rope, ensuring that the strands have been heat sealed or at least taped to stop fraying, and marry the two together with the strands interlocking with each other. Tape wrapped round this joint as a temporary measure will stop the ropes from unlaying further whilst the first tucks are made. Working on one side of the join at a time, the splicing is done in the normal way with each strand given at least three tucks. Once completed, it is a good idea to roll the rope underfoot, working the strands into place. Remember, a badly made splice will reduce the rope's strength by 50 per cent or more so it is worth taking every care.

Three strand eye splice

Rope never likes to be kinked. Where a shackle has to be used to join halyard to sail headboard, for instance, a thimble should

Fig 11: Hollow pike.
Fig 12: Swedish fid.
Fig 13: Fid.
Fig 14: Marlin pike.
Fig 15: Heaver.
Fig 16: Sharp knife.

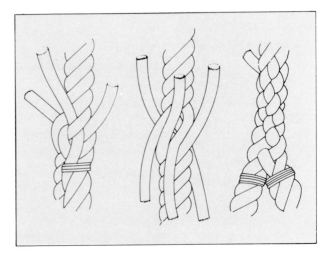

Splicing three-strand rope.

always be spliced into the rope to act both as a bearing surface for the shackle and a fair radius for the rope tail to be set round. Once the rope has been unlaid and a temporary seizing made with whipping twine to stop it from unravelling further, it can be laid round the thimble (ensure that it is of the correct size) with the loose ends ready to tuck in.

The splice is done in the usual way, with four tucks given to each strand. However, it is essential that the rope is spliced tightly round the thimble, otherwise it will fall out when under load.

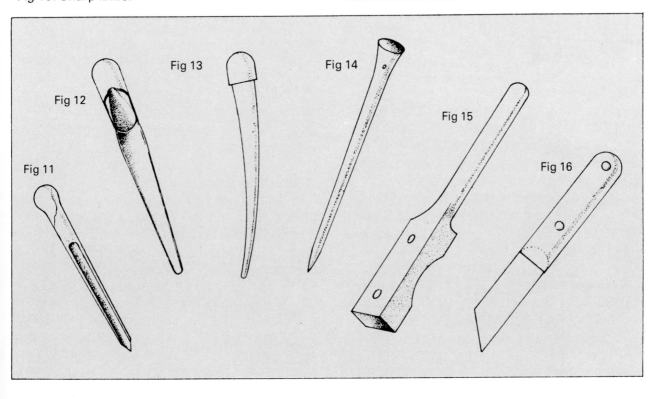

Fig 13

Fig 14

Fig 12

Fig 15

Fig 11

Fig 16

Safety Afloat

Efficient lifejackets or buoyancy aids for all onboard are a 'must' and it goes without saying that dinghy sailors should wear them at all times, whatever the weather. On cruisers, safety harnesses are sensible items to carry for those working on deck, just in case the weather turns nasty.

A wetsuit will keep a dinghy sailor warm in most conditions, even after a capsize, but cruising people will find a good set of oilskins worn over their normal sailing clothes much more suitable.

The Coastguard co-ordinates all search and rescue operations and it is this service which calls out the lifeboats, aircraft and helicopters. Search and rescue can be an expensive business. An operation involving lifeboats and helicopters should never be invoked lightly.

When calling for inshore assistance from up to three miles (5 km) out, use red hand flares and orange smoke signals. In coastal waters and offshore, red parachute rockets are easily seen. It is best to let two off within about two minutes, then wait four or five minutes before repeating the procedure. Always retain one hand flare to signal to approaching rescuers.

Every year the Coastguard service is alerted to more than 1,000 distress calls or overdue reports. More often than not they have insufficient information about the type of craft involved, equipment on board and its sailing schedule. To combat this they now operate a Yacht and Boat Safety scheme which all boat owners should join – it costs nothing and one day might well save your life. All you need do is register your craft by filling in a simple post paid card obtainable from all Coastguard stations, marinas, yacht clubs and Harbour Masters' offices.

Weather patterns can change so fast that even the experts are sometimes caught out predicting what will happen six hours ahead. However, the weather can make all the difference between an enjoyable cruise and an expensive salvage claim. When going

Above: Foul-weather oilskins.
Opposite top: Bouyancy aids should always be worn in dinghies. These need not be bulky as can be seen (*opposite below right*). Safety harnesses are a must for all those going offshore, but when in use make sure the carbine hooks are clipped to something more secure than the halyard shown in our picture (*opposite below left*).

afloat, it is very important to get an up-to-date forecast for the local area.

Each area in Britain has its own weather centre and telephones are manned round the clock to answer individual queries (telephone numbers are listed in the preface of all Post Office directories). The local Coastguard station will also provide up-to-date information and, like most harbour offices, they give a visible warning of gales by hoisting a black cone from the yardarm of their masts. The North Cone (hoisted with the point uppermost) indicates a gale from the north while the South Cone (point down) means a gale from the south.

Distress flares – what to have aboard (Check with Coastguard for latest information)

	small craft sailing within 3 miles of shore	larger craft up to 7 miles offshore	craft sailing further than 7 miles offshore
red hand flares	2	4	4
orange smoke signals	2	2	2
red parachute rockets		4	4
white hand flares (for collision warning)	2	2	2

Beaufort Wind scale

Beaufort Number	Limits of Wind Speed in knots	Descriptive Terms	Sea Criterion	Probable Height of Waves	
				feet	metres
0	Less than 1	Calm	Sea like a mirror	—	—
1	1 – 3	Light air	Ripples with the appearance of scales are formed but without foam crests.	¼	0.1
2	4 – 6	Light breeze	Small wavelets, still short but more pronounced. Crests have a glassy appearance and do not break.	½	0.2
3	7 – 10	Gentle breeze	Large wavelets. Crests begin to break. Foam of glassy appearance. Perhaps scattered white horses.	2	0.6
4	11 – 16	Moderate breeze	Small waves, becoming longer: fairly frequent horses.	3½	1
5	17 – 21	Fresh breeze	Moderate waves, taking a more pronounced long form: many white horses are formed. (Chance of some spray).	6	1.8
6	22 – 27	Strong breeze	Large waves begin to form; the white foam crests are more extensive everywhere. (probably some spray).	9½	2.8
7	28 – 33	Near Gale	Sea heaps up and white foam from breaking waves begins to be blown in streaks along the direction of the wind.	13½	4
8	34 – 40	Gale	Moderately high waves of greater length; edges of crests begin to break into spindrift. The foam is blown in well-marked streaks along the direction of the wind.	18	5.4
9	41 – 47	Strong gale	High waves. Dense streaks of foam along the direction of the wind. Crests of waves begin to topple, tumble and roll over. Spray may affect visibility.	23	6.9
10	48 – 55	Storm	Very high waves with long overhanging crests. The resulting foam in great patches is blown in dense white streaks along the direction of the wind. On the whole the surface of the sea takes a white appearance. The tumbling of the sea becomes heavy and shocklike. Visibility affected.	29	8.7

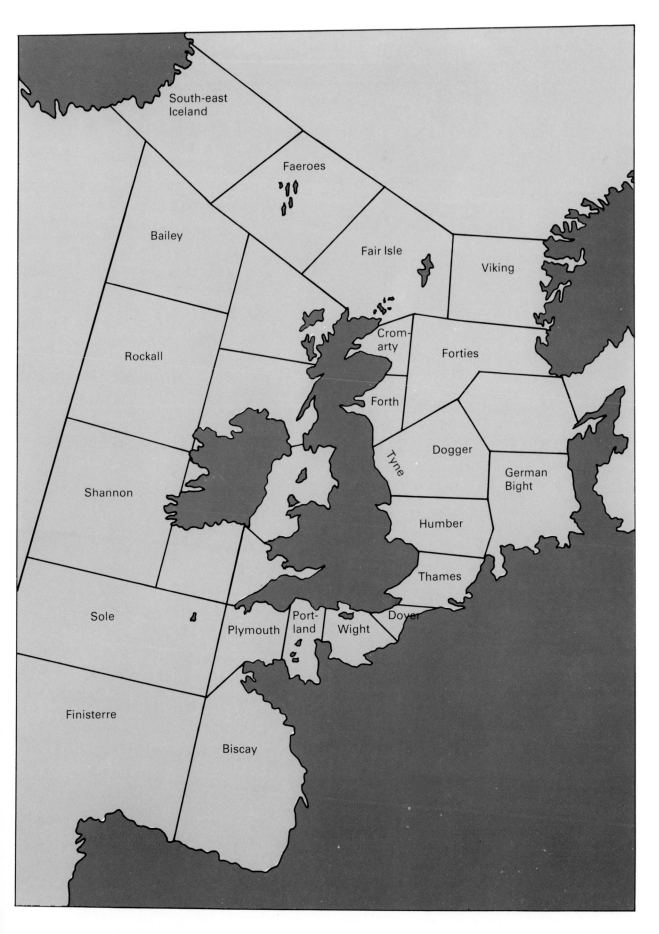

South-east
Iceland

Faeroes

Fair Isle

Viking

Bailey

Rockall

Crom-
arty

Forties

Forth

Tyne

Dogger

German
Bight

Shannon

Humber

Thames

Sole

Plymouth

Port-
land

Wight

Dover

Finisterre

Biscay

57

Rules of the Road

Many beginners believe that power should always give way to sail but this is not always the case. A fishing boat towing a trawl, for instance, is far less manoeuvrable than a yacht under sail and the latter should always give way. The same applies with deep draught vessels under power in a narrow channel.

Courtesy for other yachts is most important. At times it is common sense to keep clear, even if you have the right of way. Never speed through crowded moorings – more than one nip of rum has been lost that way! If you need to take avoiding action, do so in plenty of time in one positive move, to ensure that the other vessel is clear about your intentions. Most important, keep a watch on deck at all times.

In the dark

It will surprise you just how different even the most familiar waters look when night falls, and certainly a night sail should never be attempted until you and your crew have had a great deal of experience in daylight. Learn to differentiate between one type of boat and another. The illustrations below show some of the other lights you may see. Always ensure that your boat's lights are burning brightly so that others can see you, and be sure to keep a good look-out.

In fog, keep a sharp ear open for other

To avoid spoiling night vision, it is necessary to position lights carefully. White lights (shown here as yellow) should always be as far above or behind the helmsman as possible. Remember, port-hand lights are always red, and starboard-hand ones are always green. It is important to have lights working properly if you are going to undertake any night sailing.

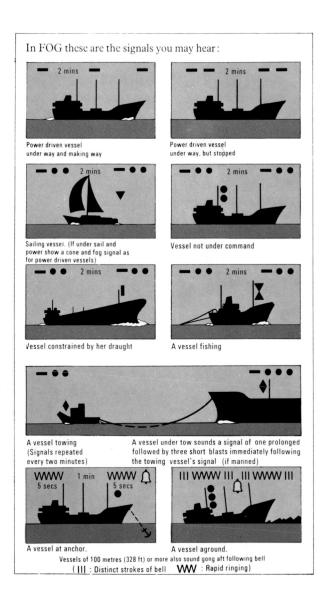

In FOG these are the signals you may hear:

Power driven vessel under way and making way

Power driven vessel under way, but stopped

Sailing vessel. (If under sail and power show a cone and fog signal as for power driven vessels)

Vessel not under command

Vessel constrained by her draught

A vessel fishing

A vessel towing (Signals repeated every two minutes)

A vessel under tow sounds a signal of one prolonged followed by three short blasts immediately following the towing vessel's signal (if manned)

A vessel at anchor.

A vessel aground.

Vessels of 100 metres (328 ft) or more also sound gong aft following bell
(||| : Distinct strokes of bell   WWW : Rapid ringing)

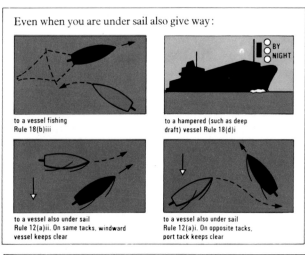

Even when you are under sail also give way:

to a vessel fishing Rule 18(b)iii

to a hampered (such as deep draft) vessel Rule 18(d)i

to a vessel also under sail Rule 12(a)ii. On same tacks, windward vessel keeps clear

to a vessel also under sail Rule 12(a)i. On opposite tacks, port tack keeps clear

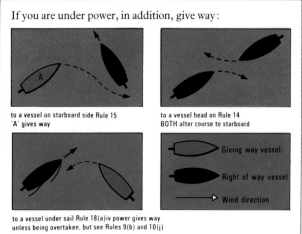

If you are under power, in addition, give way:

to a vessel on starboard side Rule 15 'A' gives way

to a vessel head on Rule 14 BOTH alter course to starboard

to a vessel under sail Rule 18(a)iv power gives way unless being overtaken, but see Rules 9(b) and 10(j)

Giving way vessel

Right of way vessel

Wind direction

SOS is the international distress signal and consists of three short dashes, then three long dashes, then three short dashes.

vessels and always be ready to take avoiding action should another craft suddenly loom out of the murk.

Buoys

Until recently many nations had their own system of marker buoys but, thankfully, most European countries at least are now changing to a universal system called the 'Maritime Buoyage System A'. This new system was first introduced in Britain in 1977 and covered an area from Newhaven to Orfordness. It was later extended to the Channel and North Sea and will finally cover all remaining coasts in the UK.

Five types of buoys are used (see overleaf) and their top marks are of particular importance, especially with the cardinal buoys since each has a particular message.

The buoyage system used in the United States of America is set out on pages 62 and 63.

Emergencies

A friend of mine was sailing through the Solent with his family on a calm summer's day. He suddenly jumped up and, without warning, threw a lifebelt overboard, informing the astonished faces aboard, who thought that they might have a severe case of sunstroke on their hands, that they had a man overboard and had better set to and recover him. He then locked himself down below and waited to see how his untried crew would cope. They managed – just – and in future will no doubt be able to react instinctively to a real emergency.

Practise the idea yourselves, taking it in

There are five types of buoy in the Maritime Buoyage System A:

Fig 1 Isolated danger marks: These are used to mark a small, isolated danger with navigable water all around. Light, white, group flashing.

Fig 2 Safe water marks: These are used in mid-channel or for landfall. Light, white, isophase, occulating or a long flash every ten seconds.

Fig 3 Cardinal marks: These are used to indicate the direction from the mark in which the best navigable water lies, or to draw attention to a bend, junction or fork in a channel, or to mark the end of a shoal. Light, always white, flashing for the four marks as follows:

(a) Continuous quick or very quick flashing.
(b) Very quick flashing (9 flashes) every ten seconds, or quick flashing (9 flashes) every fifteen seconds.
(c) Very quick flashing (3 flashes) every five seconds, or quick flashing (3 flashes) every ten seconds.
(d) Very quick flashing (6 flashes) and a long flash every ten seconds, or quick flashing (6 flashes) and a long flash every fifteen seconds.

Fig 4 Special marks: These are used to mark special points, but have no navigational significance. Light, yellow, rhythm different to any white lights on buoys.

Fig 5 Lateral marks: These are generally used to mark the sides of well-defined navigable channels. Light, red on port hand, green on starboard hand, each flashing at any rhythm.

turns on the helm. One crewman has to keep the man in sight at all times, another should throw a life buoy to him to act as a marker, and the boat should be rounded up as soon as possible. But don't put the engine into gear until you have checked that there are no ropes trailing in the water.

In a small cruiser, fire is one of the worst hazards. The engine and galley arrangements are often adjacent to the main hatch and a fire in either can make it impossible to pass through the companionway. It is always best to have at least two fire extinguishers aboard, one stored in a cockpit locker, the other just inside the forehatch ready to hand for anyone trapped below.

A Final word

In the early days don't let your ambitions exceed your experience. Take each step in easy stages. It is better to learn the basic lessons in familiar waters than suffer bad weather for the first time in unknown territory

where every landmark looks the same. When venturing out to pastures new for the first time, take an experienced hand along

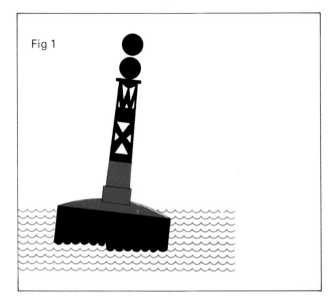

Fig 1

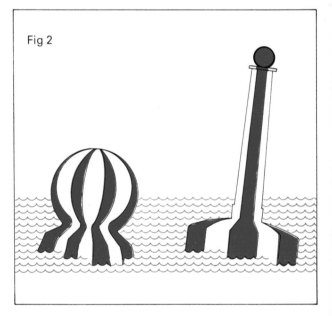

Fig 2

with you who knows the surrounding waters and can help navigate.

Always make sure that your craft is equipped with good quality (preferably Admiralty) charts of your home waters, and for cruises you may wish to make. It goes without saying that all charts on board should be amended regularly and kept up to date. There is no merit whatsoever in using an old, worn school atlas.

Finally, always respect the wind and waves. Conditions can change without warning and leave you in a wretched state.

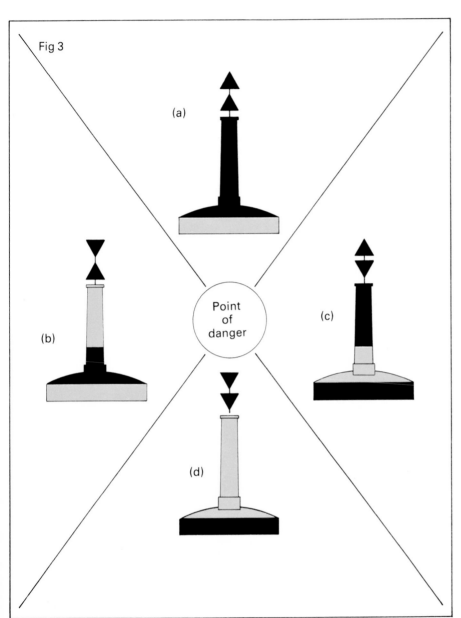

Fig 3

(a)

(b)

(c)

(d)

Point
of
danger

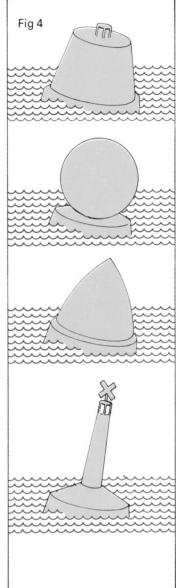

Fig 4

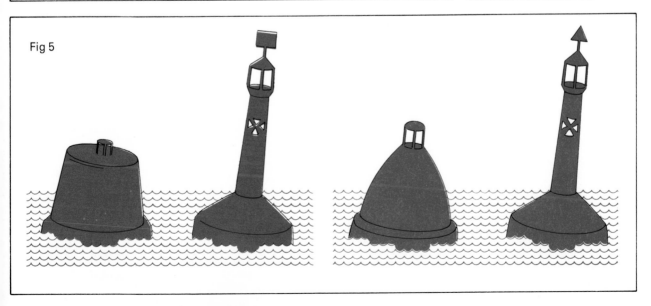

Fig 5

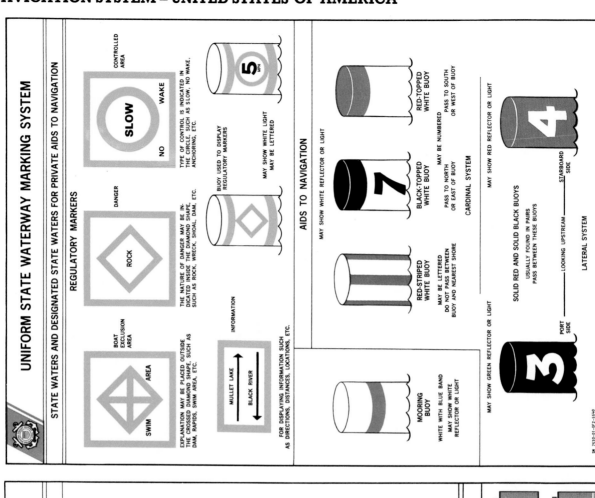

UNIFORM STATE WATERWAY MARKING SYSTEM

STATE WATERS AND DESIGNATED STATE WATERS FOR PRIVATE AIDS TO NAVIGATION

REGULATORY MARKERS

AIDS TO NAVIGATION

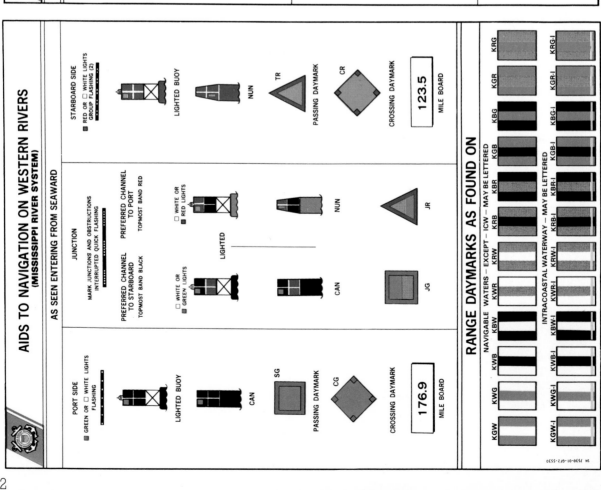

AIDS TO NAVIGATION ON WESTERN RIVERS
(MISSISSIPPI RIVER SYSTEM)

AS SEEN ENTERING FROM SEAWARD

RANGE DAYMARKS AS FOUND ON

AIDS TO NAVIGATION ON THE INTRACOASTAL WATERWAY

AS SEEN ENTERING FROM NORTH AND EAST—PROCEEDING TO SOUTH AND WEST

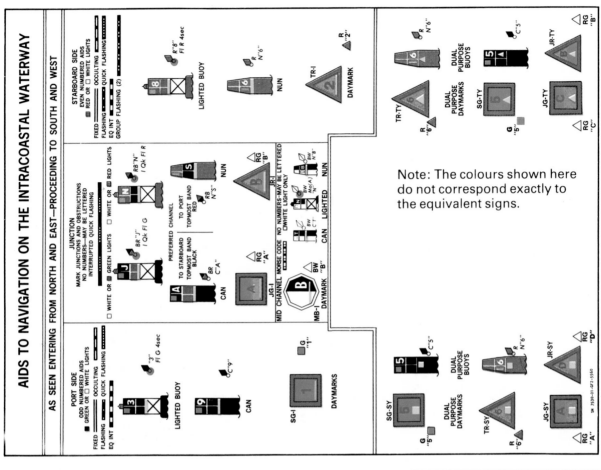

Note: The colours shown here do not correspond exactly to the equivalent signs.

AIDS TO NAVIGATION ON NAVIGABLE WATERS
except Western Rivers and Intracoastal Waterway

LATERAL SYSTEM AS SEEN ENTERING FROM SEAWARD

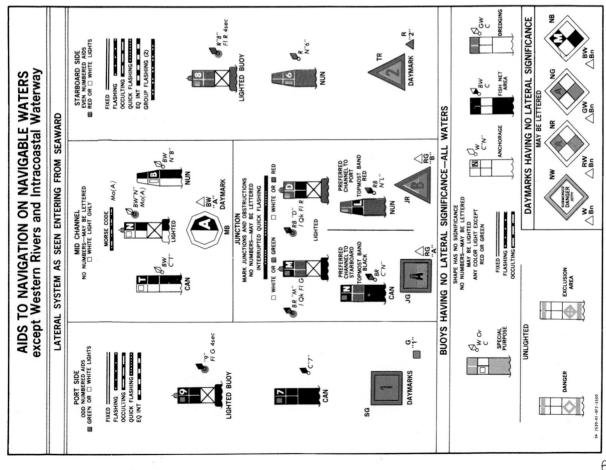

Index